RABELAIS

IN GLASGOW

Proceedings of the Colloquium held at the University of Glasgow

in December 1983.

Edited and Published by James A. Coleman and Christine M.

Scollen-Jimack, with the Support of the Department of French.

GLASGOW

1984

We wish to acknowledge the help of the University of Glasgow and of Glasgow University Library in promoting the exhibition, the conference and the present publication. We also wish to thank Dr Roderick Lyall (Dean of the Faculty of Arts) for his support, and Professors Kenneth Varty and Colin Smethurst for their valuable counsel and encouragement at all times. Finally, a special word of thanks to Ingrid Swanson, whose contribution went far beyond that of merely manipulating the word processor.

First published 1984.

Printed and bound in Glasgow by Glasgow University Printing Unit.

ISBN 0 9509831 0 1.

CONTENTS.

Clariſſimi ſacre pagine doctoris Fratris Ste
phani Bruleſer ordinis minorū in quatuor
diui ſeraphiciq; Bonauenture ſententia
rum libros interpretatio ſubtiliſſima.
Interpretatio libri primi.

Cum priuilegio.

RABELAIS IN GLASGOW

Rabelais is no stranger in Scotland: the writer and his works have been known to Scots at the very least since the time of Sir Thomas Urquhart, who referred to him as 'this learned and facetious author'. In December 1983 Glasgow University organised two events, an exhibition and a colloquium, to mark the fifth centenary of what is seen by some historians as the date of Rabelais's birth, 1483. Papers were given by seven Rabelais scholars, six from Britain and one from France, and the present volume contains the text of these papers, in some cases in revised form.

The organisers of the colloquium did not propose a specific area or theme for exploration, but since **le hasard fait bien les choses** the contributions, as it turned out, covered all four authentic books, and in their very diversity gave a remarkably representative sample of the different strands in Rabelais criticism today. The most obvious exception: there were no specifically structuralist readings of Rabelais offered; but then this might be seen as reflecting a certain resistance to this method among British **seiziémistes**. Indeed, the confrontation of different approaches, which might have seemed contradictory or mutually exclusive, was ultimately very fruitful, and served to underline the point that there is no **one** valid key to the understanding of Rabelais, but a multiplicity of possible ones, and we should use whatever means we can to try to understand an author who continues to fascinate and to puzzle.

Rabelais criticism could be seen as belonging, broadly speaking, to three different categories. The first, a textual approach, believes that Rabelais's text **is** accessible to a modern reader without his resorting to a plethora of material on the background - historical, philosophical, theological, medical, legal - and indeed that concentration on these areas is a positive hindrance to grasping the text itself. The second category, in direct opposition to the first, believes precisely that it is only through such learned apparatus that we can understand Rabelais's text, and that without this sort of 'grid' to read Rabelais, we run the danger of misreading, misunderstanding, or even simply missing the best jokes. The third category, the Bakhtinians (in a sense a variation on the second), believes that we need help in reading Rabelais, but that the help is to be found in very different areas from the learned and humanist. They concentrate on social history, popular traditions (carnival, etc.) and the popular literature which both directly influenced Rabelais, or can be seen as a written formulation of those popular traditions.

George Sutherland's paper certainly falls into the first category. Going against received wisdom in his inimitable way, he concentrates on the Enigma of Thélème, providing a powerful plea for an aesthetic (and strongly a-historical) reading of **Gargantua**. He seeks to adjust the present balance sheet on Thélème by giving Frère Jean's interpretation of the Enigma equal weight to Gargantua's, and indeed insisting very firmly on the fact that it is Frère Jean who quite literally has the last word in the book. Dorothy Coleman, in her paper on language in the **Tiers Livre**, shares many of George Sutherland's reservations about the type of Rabelais criticism which concentrates on sources or history. Her concern is above all to explore Rabelais's use of language and its impact on the reader, which she accomplishes with the same kind of sensitivity that is apparent in her critical writings on poetry. Her response to the Rabelaisian text is a deeply felt and almost physical one, and we can only regret that the mere printed page cannot do justice to the impact of her actual delivery. Ian Morrison concentrates on a close reading of some forensic episodes in **Gargantua** and in the third and fourth books, attempting to elucidate some of Rabelais's notions on justice, but looking particularly at areas of the text where eloquence in pleading (presented seriously in the Ulrich Gallet episodes or satirically in the case of Janotus and the bells) and efficacity seem to be in conflict.

On the other side of the fence we find Anthony Levi and Marie Madeleine Fontaine, using information on matters theological and medical respectively to throw light on the text. Anthony Levi explores Ficino and fifteenth-century Florentine neo-platonism in order to discuss the attitudes of Rabelais (and other sixteenth-century writers) to man's capacity for goodness and the problem of free will. For him, Rabelais's use of a highly demotic form is in fact a way of smuggling in vital new theological notions, without running the risk of condemnation for heresy. Marie Madeleine Fontaine, in discussing the description of Quaresmeprenant (**Quart Livre**, 30-32), rejects such notions as **délire verbal**, and insists that the lists and comparisons in these chapters can most usefully be considered against the background of contemporary medical debate. In this instance we need to understand something of the long-standing discussion about the validity, or otherwise, of using analogy in describing anatomical features, and the search for alternative systems of representation by Vesalius and others. But her thesis goes further, and she points out that in the Renaissance the status of the image in both medicine and literature is modified, and in comparable ways.

From the learned to the popular. Carol Clark and John Parkin are both primarily concerned with the 'Vulgar Rabelais', to borrow the title of Carol Clark's recent book, in which she freely acknowledges the debt that she and the whole younger generation of Rabelais critics owe to Bakhtin's **Rabelais and his World.** Both Carol Clark and John Parkin are interested in social history, in carnival and other sixteenth-century manifestations of licensed folly. The former concentrates on attitudes to fools and folly, looking at texts and iconographical material from a wide range of sources (from Erasmus and his imitators to the **sermons joyeux** associated with fool societies). All this throws light on many aspects of Rabelais's work, but more particularly on the role and function of Panurge, which is precisely what pre-occupies John Parkin. His discussion of the alternative value systems which prevailed during periods of carnival or other festivity focusses specifically on the rough justice meted out to individuals in various episodes of **Pantagruel** and the **Quart Livre,** and inevitably entails a long look at Panurge.

What is very striking about the papers viewed as whole is that despite the multiplicity of approaches, critics tend to concentrate on similar areas. Although John Parkin and Ian Morrison differ widely in their methodology (and many of their conclusions) they both share some preoccupations about Rabelais and justice, including the assumption that Rabelais did indeed believe in a transcendent moral order, but recognises the problems involved in the administration of justice by mere mortals.

Yet again, it is clear that discussion of the Thélème episode has not yet been exhausted. Anthony Levi's paper insists on the value of exploring the discussion on free will by Rabelais's predecessors and contemporaries, but this does not lead him to propose a single exclusive interpretation of the episode. He remarks very sagaciously that the Thélème episode 'preserves its perfect multivalency'. Anti-monastery with Renaissance trappings: ostentatiously Renaissance utopian society: forthright attack on Luther using terms borrowed from Erasmus - we are invited to take our pick. George Sutherland's remarks on the Enigma take us in a rather different direction, for he is above all concerned to free the text from the framework of theology. However, he too is surely arguing for a plurality of readings of Rabelais's text, for it is not **either** Gargantua **or** Frère Jean, but **both** Gargantua **and** Frère Jean who are right. Rabelais is not a closed text, but an ever open one.

But of all the topics discussed, the most frequently recurring one was the nature and function of Panurge. Anthony Levi simply remarks in passing that 'in Panurge was recognised a parody of Odysseus'. Dorothy Coleman's remarks on the **Tiers Livre** present him not as a figure satirised for his **philautia**, but quite simply as a pivotal comic figure, the mainspring of the action, a view endorsed by both Carol Clark and John Parkin. Indeed, the latter remarks that the comic dynamism of Panurge is never in fact defeated in the course of the **Tiers Livre** by the normative wisdom of Pantagruel. The understanding of this often puzzling and sometimes repulsive figure is perhaps most helped by a Bakhtinian approach. Carol Clark sees him as a (wise) fool, whose role is often akin to that of the court jester. John Parkin insists above all on Panurge as a type. In his remarks on the episode of Panurge and the Parisian lady (**Pantagruel**, 21-22) he stresses the dangers of misreading if we try to view him as an individual with psychological motivation, belonging to a much later fictional tradition. Panurge is not a thug or a sadist, he is a **jeunesse** leader enacting a travesty of courtship, and subsequently visiting on the lady a recognisable carnivalesque punishment for a potential adulteress.

A final perennial question, all the more intriguing because it is virtually unanswerable – who read Rabelais, and how much did they understand? Dorothy Coleman poses it at the very beginning of her paper: 'How many of his own contemporaries understood **Le Tiers Livre**? Certain scholars would say all the élite. I think that it is still an unanswered question.' Anthony Levi goes even further. In stressing the strange mixture of learned allusions and demotic French that makes up Rabelais's works, he suggests that the only person who could have fully understood Rabelais was the writer himself ' . . . Rabelais almost systematically fills his books with hidden erudite allusions primarily to amuse and parody himself, but perhaps also to declare his humanist literary parentage. It was a learned and elegant game . . . ' And while both Carol Clark and John Parkin are much concerned with the popular origins of Rabelais, popular origins do not necessarily entail a popular audience; however, evidence might suggest that Rabelais was widely known if not always carefully read and fully understood.

Be that as it may, the colloquium certainly proved to be a gathering of careful readers of Rabelais, and if their readings did not always coincide, they provided a feast of ideas and posed some fascinating questions. We were left to drink from Rabelais's **inexpuisable tonneau** ourselves and ultimately to read (or as some critics would have it) write our own book.

Last, but not least, a special word of thanks is due to Stephen Rawles of Glasgow University Library, who not only conceived the original idea of both the exhibition and the colloquium, but who

also carried out most of the major tasks involved in the
organisation of these two events with exemplary efficiency and
unfailing energy.

Christine M. Scollen-Jimack

Pantagruel,

Roy des Dipsodes, restitue
son naturel, auec ses faictz
& proüesses espouenta
bles: cōposez par feu
M. Alcofribas
abstracteur
de quinte
essence.

M. D. XLII.

On les vend a Lyon chez Francoys
Juste, deuāt nře Dame de Cōfort.

RABELAIS IN GLASGOW UNIVERSITY LIBRARY

The idea for a Rabelais Colloquium was born out of an exhibition of books in Glasgow University Library organised by Stephen Rawles. The exhibition, which ran from 28th November 1983 to 13th January 1984, revealed the richness of the Glasgow collections: some seventy items by Rabelais or associated with him were chosen for display. Title pages of the more interesting items (asterisked) are reproduced on pages 4, 10, 12, 54, 86 and 144.

The first section of the exhibition was devoted to Rabelais's fiction itself: the very rare 1534 Juste edition of **Pantagruel***; the 1542 edition* with **Gargantua** from the same press; several sixteenth century Lyons editions of the complete works; a counterfeit **Gargantua** from ca. 1600; both Elzevier editions; and Le Duchat's critical edition of 1711.

Next came a unique opportunity to see together the three editions (1532*, 1543*, 1545) of works of Hippocrates and Galen edited by Rabelais.

A further section reconstituted a part of Rabelais's own library, with editions identical to those he worked from, while titles which once figured in the genuine catalogue of the Bibliothèque Saint Victor were displayed beside the originals of several items parodied in Rabelais's comic catalogue (**Pantagruel**, chapter 7):

Pantofla Decretorum ...
Tartaretus de modo cacandi ...
Majoris de arte faciendi boudinos* ...
Politronismus rerum italicum autore magistro Bruslefer* ...
R. Lullius de batisfolagiis principium ...
De auferibilitate pape ab ecclesia ...
Les henilles de Gaietan ...

The final sections of the exhibition comprised works connected with both phases of Gargantua's education, with the **Tiers Livre** (especially the folly of Panurge and the mock encomium), and with the voyage and storm of the **Quart Livre.**

HIPPO
CRATIS AC GA=
leni libri aliquot, ex recognitio
ne Francisci Rabelæsi, medici
omnibus numeris absolutissi=
mi : quoru‿ elenchum se
quens pagella indi
cabit.

Hic medicæ fons est exundantissimus artis.
Hinc, mage ni sapiat pigra lacuna, bibe.

VIRTVTE DVCE,   CÖMITE FORT.

Apud Gryphium Lugd.
1532
c

THE RABELAISIAN SEE-SAW
SOME REMARKS ON THE ENIGMA OF THELEME

George Sutherland

The **Enigme trouvé es fondemens de l'abbaye des Thelemites**
having been read, we now hear this:

La lecture de cestuy monument parachevée, Gargantua souspira
profondément et dit es assistans: 'Ce n'est pas de maintenant que
les gentz reduictz à la creance Evangelicque sont persecutez; mais
bien heureux est celluy qui ne sera scandalizé et qui tousjours
tendra au but, au blanc que Dieu, par son Cher Enfant, nous a
prefix, sans par ses affections charnelles estre distraict ny
diverty.'
Le Moyne dist: 'Que pensez vous, en vostre entendement, estre
par cest enigme designé et signifié?
— Quoy? (dist Gargantua). Le decours et maintien de verité
divine.
— Par sainct Goderan (dist le Moyne), je pense que c'est la
description du jeu de paulme, et que la **machine ronde** est l'esteuf,
et ces **nerfs et boyaulx de bestes innocentes** sont les racquestes, et
ces gentz eschauffez et debatans sont les joueurs. La fin est que
apres avoir bien travaillé, ilz s'en vont repaistre; et grand
chiere!'[1]

My aim in this paper is a modest one: by an old-fashioned
lecture expliquée of this page I hope to show, first, that nothing
Gargantua says or does here may be used in order to establish, or to
suggest however tentatively, a date of composition or publication
for this book, or any part of it; and, second, after two or three
others but in my own way, to show that Frere Jean's words are just
as important as Gargantua's: not more important, although no doubt
more difficult in the making, nor less important, but just as
important. **Optons toujours choses médiocres.** He is on the other
end of the see-saw, and to remove him from there is **eo ipso** to
destroy the meaning of the last page, and, by artistic inference and
implication, to destroy also the meaning of the Enigma, of the
episode of Thélème together with its **Inscription,** of every other
péripétie in the book, and lastly of the whole sphere or gyre itself
which is called **Gargantua,** and for which this last page forms the
only correct, appropriate, and condign **clausula, et couvercle digne
du chaudron.** For the whole is prior to the part, and the form must

be closed before it can be opened, **quoi qu'en disent ou quoi qu'en fassent la logique et la raison raisonnante.**

Nothing is more finely observed than the perfect balance which Gargantua establishes between, on the one hand, his sympathy and compassion for those who presently suffer, expressed by his **soupir profond**, and, on the other hand, his immediate detachment, in his very first words, from the **punctum temporis** of sorrow and its placing by him **sub specie aeternitatis** - to coin a phrase - of the lively oracles of God. The words **Ce n'est pas de maintenant** are **translatés** by Demerson/Intégrale/Seuil as 'ce n'est pas d'aujourd'hui', and we will not quarrel with that. After all this **Enigme**, having been dug up from the foundations, is like the 'penniless lass wi' a lang pedigree', and goes back a long long way; and inasmuch as it is an **Enigme en Prophétie** it goes forward a long way as well. It is like the oak of La Fontaine

> Celui de qui la tête au ciel était voisine
> Et dont les pieds touchaient à l'empire des morts;

and both dimensions, of looking before and after, are summed up beautifully in the single word **monument**, which is at once a reminding and a foretelling, with a warning thrown in **pour renfort de potage.**

This is not the first time, then, and by implication it will not be the last time, **que les gentz reduictz à la creance Evangelicque** etc., for the sufferings of the persecuted **dans la bonne cause** we will always have with us, always in Rama will there be a voice heard, of Rachel weeping for her children, and will not be comforted because they are not. In these first words Gargantua pushes out, as it were, into the ocean, and of course there will be sorrow there, nobody knows that better than those **qui sont reduictz à la creance Evangelicque,** but it is the ocean of God's mercy, God's goodness, God's grace, God's joy and God's truth.

The second sentence **Mais bien heureux est celluy . . .** is another decisive step away from the present moment, while not forgetting it for an instant; and this step, heralded as it is and made manifest by the simple adversative conjunction **Mais,** continues with a superlative epithet. For **bien heureux** is **heureux in excelsis, felicissimus;** cf. **le roi très-chrétien, rex christianissimus** - and that's a joke if ever there was one. Now the thrust of this sentence is in these words **bien heureux est celluy** which is the principal clause, to which the other clauses, although of course important in their own right, are nonetheless subordinate. Gargantua is not saying to these **assistans,** who are his audience in this amphitheatre

Conticuere omnes intentique ora tenebant[2]

- he is not saying 'There is a great need for you to keep, at this moment in time, the very stiffest of stiff upper lips, in view of all those **placards** flying about **un peu partout, et jusque sur la porte de la chambre du roi très-chrétien lui-même, quelle horreur! proh pudor!** Ichabod, Ichabod, and sundry other exclamations **de même farine**, on the night of the 17th-18th October 1534, or alternatively the 13th-14th January 1535 (**nouveau style, doit-on préciser, dans l'un et l'autre cas**), take your pick, **on n'a que l'embarras du choix**'. This is not a serious call, and it is not a tragic injunction; it is a blessing and a benediction. He's about to start on a mini-sermon on the Mount, and this is a Gargantuan Beatitude: **Blessed are ye, when men shall revile you and persecute you, and shall say all manner of evil against you falsely, for my sake. Rejoice and be exceeding glad; for so persecuted they the prophets which were before you.** The emphasis of Gargantua, like the emphasis in the last lines of the Enigma, in all editions, is one with the emphasis of Jesus, and is of an impeccable, Alpha-to-Omega and from-the-eggs-to-the-apples orthodoxy.

It is at this point that Frere Jean becomes alarmed, and says to himself in dismay: 'Here we go again, here's another long tirade coming up **à la Ulrich Gallet**, another **concion es vaincuz**, another huge **morceau de rhetoricque ciceroniane**, et je l'ai assez vu; I must stop him now, before he goes any further, otherwise we'll all be here all night and we'll never get to our beds'. So he asks Gargantua plump and plain, and with that easy, unquestioning and unquestioned assumption of intimacy which is the lovely heart and centre of Rabelaisian **amitié, cet incomparable auteur de l'art de conférer**: 'Que pensez vous, en vostre entendement, estre par cest enigme designé et signifié?' i.e. 'Would you please cut the cackle, **mon ami**, stop beating about the burning bush, and come straight to the point: what do you make of this puzzle, this **Enigme**?' And Gargantua, interrupted in the full flow of his **facundia**, his **os magna soniturum**, says **Quoy? Le decours et maintien de verité divine.**

Now it is important to note that these words **Le decours et maintien de verité divine** are the only **words** which specifically represent Gargantua's reading of the Enigma, given by him in reply to Frere Jean's direct question **à brûle-pourpoint**. All his other **words**, from **Ce n'est pas de maintenant** to the interrogative/exclamatory **Quoy?** inclusive, are mere starters, hors d'oeuvre, **préambule**, and prolegomena. He heaves a deep sigh, **d'accord, et je** ne dis pas le contraire; and, judging by that long sprawling adverb **profondément,** I daresay none of these **assistans** will ever forget it; but the sigh, even of a Gargantua, **voyons,** since it is pre-linguistic, extra-linguistic, a- ab- abs- ex- and e-linguistic, has no more semantic significance than the cry of an infant in the night

> An infant crying for the light
> And with no language but a cry.

His sigh is on the far side of the gulf which divides sentence from speech, the differentia of man, **animal symbolicum.**[3]

But before I deal with **Le decours et maintien**...let me say something about **Quoy?** which precedes it. This **Quoy?** has a triple function: first, it means, it implies, that Gargantua is surprised in the middle of his discourse, since the words **Le Moyne dist,** at the head of the phrase, simulate, so to speak, the physical halting, by Frere Jean, of the oracular advance of Gargantua. Later, when the crisis is past, the phrase which contains the **verbum dicendi** can take its usual place, with its elements trajected, several syllables into the sentence. Next, this surprise is the equivalent of the question which, by means of the **Quoy?** Gargantua is himself putting to Frere Jean, i.e. 'Isn't it obvious what the meaning of this Enigma must be? Need you ask? It's as plain as the nose on your face'. And, finally, its abrupt exclamatory nature injects a note of comicality **in medias res gravissimas,** a comicality which is increased by the contemporary pronunciation of the word, like a half-shut knife mid-way between the vertical and the horizontal, thus: [kwɛ] .

Now, as to the meaning of the words **Le decours et maintien de verité divine,** they make up an exclusively nominal phrase, having no verb anywhere; but the meaning of the three nouns **decours, maintien, verité,** in their accusative/genitival stitching together, is such that all tenses of the verb **to be,** past present and to come, are sucked up into and implied in their massive substantiality. **Decours:** this goes right back past the New Testament to the book of Genesis and the LORD GOD walking in the garden in the cool of the day, and forward to the same LORD GOD in that day when he cometh to make up his jewels. As for **maintien,** this means that every moment of that time is safe and secure from all alarms, there is no weak link anywhere in the golden chain of God's truth and his freedom. For ye shall know the truth, says his **cher Enfant,** and the truth shall make you free. The line is the precise Rabelaisian equivalent of the last two lines of one of the glories of the Scottish psalter

All people that on earth do dwell, the 'Old Hundredth':

> His truth at all times firmly stood,
> And shall from age to age endure;

and the source and origin of both of them is, of course, the last words of that same Psalm 100: 'his truth endureth to all generations', **Le decours et maintien de verité divine.** The truth is his, and his alone, and only he maintains it. All that we **homunculi** and **mulierculae** have to do is to abide by it and to revere it.

Since therefore it is an indissoluble amalgam of truth and freedom, the line possesses immense power and majesty, and is fully able to be the fulcrum of this see-saw, able easily to bear the weight of fifty Gargantuas at one end of it, and of five hundred Frere Jeans (or Freres Jean) at the other, each and all of them raising aloft, and preparing to lay about him with the **baston de la croix.**

Now if it is not possible to refer the previous sentence, or the sentence before that again, to the sufferings of the contemporary **Evangéliques,** it is even more impossible to do so here, if such things exist as degrees of impossibility. Before we can make of these twelve syllables, this **alexandrin en disponibilité,** a call, a plea, or a command - for this is the current and received wisdom, this is the thesis in residence - or an order, an injunction or a warning to persist in resisting persecution,[4] we shall simply have to supply a verb, and this verb cannot just be any old verb. It will have to be either an imperative or a subjunctive, a jussive, optative, or hortatory subjunctive; but such a verb is to be found nowhere in any of Gargantua's words, or in any of those of the Enigma either, which are governed throughout by the indicative mood: 'these things have been, these things are, and these things shall be'; and least of all in what is given specifically as Gargantua's account of the Enigma, which is, instead, a calm and authoritative assurance, in that note of euphoria and heartsease, to which all the prophets join their several and united voices: 'He that dwelleth in the secret place of the most High shall abide under the shadow of the Almighty', which is 'the shadow of a great rock in a weary land'. 'The eternal GOD is thy refuge, and underneath are the everlasting arms'. 'The LORD bless thee and keep thee: The LORD make his face shine upon thee and be gracious unto thee; The LORD lift up his countenance upon thee, and give thee peace'. It is an affirmation plainly in the major key, **et il faut n'avoir point d'oreille pour ne pas l'entendre,** that key of C major which we associate with the world of **Gargantua** despite all the suffering portrayed therein. For the Enigma is retrospective as well as prospective, and Gargantua's words of refulgent grace are those of the philosopher-king who does not forget the perils through which his people have passed in the **guerre picrocholine.** Besides, surely we are not going to limit the humanity and compassion of Rabelais, of all people under Heaven of François Rabelais, the bard who present past and future sees, to the concern which he rightly feels, who denies it? for his immediate contemporaries **les Evangéliques des Placards?** For he that loveth not his brother whom he hath seen, how can he love God, whom he hath not seen? **C'est une grande question, dit Candide.**

Let us be on our guard against that linguistic-cum-logical error which is called **petitio principii,** i.e. of assuming, as already proved, that which has not been proved, has still to be proved, **et dont il faudra renvoyer la preuve aux calendes grecques ou bien à la venue des cocquecigrues;** in this case, of assuming that, when Gargantua says **les gentz reduictz à la creance Evangelicque** he means or implies, no matter how faintly, how much **dans le filigrane** - and this **filigrane,** believe me, has a great deal to answer for, **malheureux filigrane que je te veux de mal!** - he must mean **les Evangéliques de 1534-1535, les Evangéliques des Placards.** For, in the first place, the phrase **les gentz reduictz à la creance Evangelicque,** although nominal in form, is pronominal in effect, and as such it has a high degree of built-in diffuseness and generality, tending much more therefore to the a-temporal and the a-historical, **pace les historiens, édition critique, édition Plattard, édition Jourda, édition Screech.**[5] In the second place, the word **évangélique,** adjective, goes back, in French usage, to the fourteenth century; in meaning, of course, it goes back to him who first announced and was the good news, and forward 'till a' the seas gang dry and the rocks melt wi' the sun', or **usque in consummationem saeculi,** whichever of these contingencies we may feel to be the more remote. In the third place, the word **Evangélique,** substantive, **un grand Evangélique, un Evangélique de grandeur moyenne, ou un petit Evangélique,** occurs nowhere in **Gargantua,** nor, **sauf erreur,** anywhere else in the whole of Rabelais, not even in the debatable Fifth Book. But let us first secure within us Book No 1, 2, 3, or 4 **et ne fût-ce que cette page-ci,** before we tangle with Book Five in the question 'Le **Cinquiesme Livre** de Rabelais est-il bien de Rabelais? Est-il, oui ou non, authentique?' - **faux-problème, question en porte-à-faux, s'il en fut jamais.** And in the fourth, and most important place of all, words **mean,** they do not point. If in their essence they pointed, I could not be sitting here just now reading this paper, but munching grass on all fours like Nebuchadnezzar around the

University flag-pole; except that, if indeed language were essentially apodictic, there could be no University either, let alone a flag-pole, **et quant à Nabuchodonosor, il deviendrait ce qu'il pourrait.**

Turning now to Frere Jean, I should like to begin by putting before you two simple, obvious, irrefutable **facts:** (i) that he has the last word in all editions of **Gargantua;** and (ii) that he has 55 last words in Edition A, and 152 last words in Edition E, **la dernière revue et corrigée par l'auteur, et il n'y a qu' à compter.** Gargantua's speech, on the other hand, is almost one hundred per cent identical in all editions, with but two trivial alterations between A and E: in the first of these, the **pas** is omitted from **Ce n'est pas de maintenant,** which leaves us pretty much where we were; and, in the second, **son cher Enfant** of Edition A becomes, in E, **son cher Filz,** which again makes very little odds, **puisqu' enfin il faut être fils de quelqu'un,** n'est-ce pas? and as for **Filz/Enfant, Enfant/Filz, eh oui, rôti, bouilli, même chose.**

From these facts certain large consequences will instantly and inevitably flow: if Rabelais gives Frere Jean the last words in Edition A, and almost three times as many in E, he must mean us to take this seriously, **vérité de la Pallice.** Otherwise, why have so many University teachers of French the world over been paid good money, folding money, in order that they might explicate someone who doesn't know what he's doing, and is unfit to be trusted with the key of his own front door, **bref,** an eejit? Alternatively, if Gargantua's words are the only ones which really count on this last page - and here again we come hard up against the accredited dogma, the authorised version **quae imprimatur neve in saecula saeculorum varietur**[6] - why, in that case, did not Rabelais/Alcofribas give **him** the last words, **ultima verba** always being **importantissimes?** For Rabelais could easily, had he so wished, (since we do not doubt his power), have made Gargantua say, after Frere Jean's **grand chiere!** what Pantagruel says to Panurge after the story of Soeur Fessue **Vous ja ne m'en ferez rire,**[7] and go again into his spiel about the **cher Enfant,** the bit about **Le decours et maintien de verité divine,** and all that. But this never happens. Now if he does not disagree with Frere Jean, Gargantua must in some sense, which it is our task, nay our sacred duty, to tease out and explicate, he must in some sense agree with him, he that is not against him being necessarily for him, 2e **vérité de la Pallice.** Nor has the almost three-fold increase in Frere Jean's words, or the alterations to the Enigma itself, anything whatever to do with changes in the historical situation in the seven years which elapse between 1535 and 1542. Every period of seven years, **pour peu qu'on y réfléchisse,** since ever there have been periods of seven years, resembles every other one **comme deux soeurs, deux soeurs d'ailleurs fort peu ragoûtantes,** and I would again refer you to Gargantua's first words. Of each and all of such **septennia** we can say what was said about the then Prince of Wales, whose health, or lack of it, was giving some cause for concern at the end of the nineteenth century:

> Along the wires the electric message came:
> 'He is no better, he is much the same'.

Now while Gargantua's job is simply to keep the balance even between **nunc** and the two **olims,** the truth of God which is the same yesterday today and forever, Rabelais has given to Frere Jean his **jongleur de Notre Dame bien avant la lettre** several balls to play with in the air at once; and it would be easy for us, as spectators, simply to revel in the sheen and effulgence of this pure appearance, this manifold epiphany

> Next when I cast mine eyes and see
> That brave vibration each way free
> O how that glittering taketh me!

especially if we bear in mind the wise saying of Paul Valéry 'L'oeuvre d'art n'existe qu'en acte', and the equally wise saying of Wolfgang Amadeus Mozart 'If my music pleases you, then what pleases me most is your silent applause'. But, as it is, I am here proposing to stop all these balls in their spins and gyrations, and to describe each one of them as best I can; thereby combining in myself a would-be squarer of the circle, **un chercheur de midi à quatorze heures,** and Dr Johnson's dog standing on its hinder legs, the surprising thing about which is not that it is done well, but that it should be done at all. Incidentally, and entirely by the way, why was there so very, very little literary-criticism in the Renaissance? Is it because they knew so much less than we do, or so much more than we do? And what would Montaigne have made of a deconstructionist? (These are all rhetorical questions, which do not expect any answer.)

Surveying then our balls in ascending order of importance, **puisque nous sommes, hélas! les gens de maintenant,** the first of them will represent the traditional demand that the **mot de l'énigme** shall be either trivial or scabrous, or better still, why not? **et n'en déplaise à Madame Marie Maison Blanche,** a combination of both. The monk's interpretation is trivial **à volonté,** although one will look in vain, I think, for the scabrous in it. The second ball, showing us a game of tennis, is one of Aristotelian congruity, **c'est de l'Aristote tout craché,** since it is faithful to the known character of Frere Jean, who is all active energetic brawn - **jamais je ne suis oisif** - and but mediocre brain. Such a strenuous game seems ideally suited to a man of his vigorous nature, and we can be sure that, if he were to engage in it, and were unable to find a **racquete** lying handy, he would, in default, pick up and wield his **baston de la croix** to such purpose and effect as would even wipe the scowl off the face of J.P. McEnroe himself - or perhaps put it back on.

Next we come to **grand chiere!**, an expression which can not have figured in too many traditional **mots d'énigme**, an expression which, outside **Gargantua,** is perfectly trite, humdrum, and commonplace, but here, at the very end of this book, having all the concentrated force and triumphant meaning of the great crashing **fortissimo** chords at the end of Beethoven's Fifth Symphony. It may well have been sown in weakness, but here it has been raised in power. For the words **grand chiere!** are not the last two words in a linear longitudinal sequence, but the bringing of the wheel full circle, and the sending of it spinning into limitless orbit, its artificer retiring, like James Joyce's artist-god, to pare his finger-nails[8] - although we have, I think, the right to expect Rabelais to be doing something just a little more robust than that.

Grand chiere! has the eyes of Argus, and looks in several directions at once: first, to the players in that game of tennis which is all that Frere Jean sees in the Enigma, then to Gargantua himself, swinging away there at the other end of the see-saw; next, to the **assistans, ceux qui se trouvaient là,** as Demerson's **translation** has it, prudently hedging all its bets. Who exactly are these **assistans**? Was there ever a word more beautifully vague? **Curiosa Rabelaisi felicitas,**[9] indeed. Finally, in its temper, its ethos, for it is powerful metaphor and the leit-motif of the entire book, **grand chiere!** looks straight through the centre of the sphere to the first, but the very first words of Alcofribas in the Prologue: **Beuveurs tresillustres, et vous Verolés tresprecieux - car à vous, non à aultres, sont dediez mes escreptz.** The hapless Mary Queen of Scots, before the block at Fotheringay, said **En ma fin est mon commencement,** and so it is with this book, 'it cam' wi' a **beuveur** and it'll gang wi' a' **beuveur**'; and where, among all the thousands who throng its pages, will you find a more **illustre beuveur** and guzzler, a **Verolé** more **precieux** than Frere Jean, a man of wine **du vin divin,** and not of oil, and living one million light-years away, at a modest computation, from the man with the muck-rake?

Rabelais has many backgrounds - **paulo enim maiora canamus**[10] - and thousands upon thousands of sources; he can say with Phèdre

> J'ay pour ayeul le pere et le maistre des dieux
> Le ciel tout l'univers est plein de mes ayeulx

but of all of these the most important by far is the Bible, since long before this religious by conviction and profession publishes a single syllable of his creative work, very near the end of his tenth lustre, the age, in Renaissance terms, of **le bon père Anchise sur les épaules de son fils**

> Ja dix lustres passés et ja mon poil grison
> M'appellent au logis et sonnent la retraite[11]

- long before this its great passages have become his **sang et nourriture,** bone of his bones and flesh of his flesh, his very glance and gesture; for

> It's a very odd thing
> As odd as can be
> That whatever Miss T. eats
> Turns into Miss T;[12]

and in my view the last seven chapters of **Gargantua** are all thematically linked, they are all written under the impregnating shadow of St Matthew's Gospel, chapter 25 and verses 31-46, that vision of the last things in which the sheep are divided from the goats, in which the blessed of the Father are summoned to inherit the Kingdom prepared for them from the foundation of the world, but the others are bidden to depart into everlasting fire. For the great theme of judgment-cum-election, election-cum-judgment, strikes, in these last chapters, in four separate places, although in each case with a different index of artistic refraction: the prose chapters of Thélème, the **Inscription,** the Enigma itself, and, in a manner wholly implicit as far as Frere Jean is concerned, and which therefore will need some unravelling, the last page of all where Gargantua and Frere Jean offer their different solutions of the Enigma.   Thélème is obviously given as a **lieu d'élection,** a superior finishing-school for **la crème de la crème** albeit with a strong ethico-spiritual flavour; the **Inscription mise sus la grande porte** is Rabelais's gothic rendition of the same text; the Enigma adds to the theme of predestination the apocalyptic-eschatological note; the rivalling interpretations, I shall argue, present us with the two people who are the real **élus** of Rabelais in this book, those who are, in the words of Louis Jouvet as he cries up and drums up custom for his indulgences in the film **La Kermesse héroïque**, 'les seuls authentiques, les seuls contrôlés'.

I do not need to go over again the ground which has been so brilliantly covered by François RIGOLOT [13], good name, **felix opportunitate nominis, et si cet homme-là n'eût point existé, il eût fallu l'inventer.** I'd just like to say, in the context of the thematic linking which I have suggested, that while Thélème may well be a **conceptual** paradise, it is a **perceptual** Hades, or at any rate no place for real individuals to live in. By the gorgeous vestments which he gives them Rabelais covers up all the bodies of the Thélémites; in fact the only bodies one sees there are those of the three Graces in the fountain, **pierres mortes** which are yet much more **vives** than those of any of the inhabitants, if only because of all that water gushing perpetually out **par les mamelles, bouches, aureilles, oieulx, et aultres ouvertures du corps,** whatever they might be; and what, in this **ambiance,** would we not give for the **roupie** depending from Frere Jean's proboscis, abnormally elongated as it is **pour la raison que l'on sait?** But what is much more serious is that we don't see any of their souls or minds or spirits either. The **raison théologienne** of a Martin Luther can play about as much as it likes, let Luther have his swink to him reserved, with the conceptual paradoxes of the **Chrestien tres libre, seigneur de tous, sujet à nul, ... tres serviable, serviteur de tous, sujet à tous;**[14] but the effect made upon us by chapter 55 of **Gargantua** is very different. **Peindre, non la chose,** says Stéphane Mallarmé, **mais l'effet qu'elle produit.** (In this whole episode, by the way, people are heavily outnumbered by things, but literature is pre-eminently about people, since from Homer to Jean Genet and from Lucretius to Samuel Beckett **de nobis solum semper et ubique fabula narratur,** and the proper study of mankind is man.)

The injunction **Fay ce que vouldras,** addressed as it is to a single person, looks very strange indeed, a strangeness compounded by typography whether italics or block capitals, in the middle of all those clotted and coagulated plurals; and even such singulars as do occur are shown to us **sous le voile de l'anonyme,** silent, in a bathysphere 10,000 leagues under the ocean, **véritable cathédrale engloutie: nul ne les eveilloit, nul ne les parforceoyt ny à boire ny à manger ... si quelqu'un ou quelqu'une disoit: 'Beuvons', tous beuvoient; si disoit: 'Jouons', tous jouoient; si disoit: 'Allons à l'esbat es champs', tous y alloyent.**[15] Whatever happened to the 'incomparable auteur de l'art de conférer'? When this phantasmal Father or Mother, this **vox et praeterea nihil** says 'Turn', they all turn; they're all doing their own thing, **d'accord**, but they're all doing the same thing, together and at once, all 932 of them - 9332 at the last count; and if it wasn't for the pejorative note in these lines from **King Lear** they would apply not too badly to the Thélémites, who

> Renege affirm and turn their halcyon beaks
> With every gale and vary of their masters.

The repeated plurals produce in the end a multiple **stasis** of all those still unravished brides of quietness - and unravished bridegrooms as well, for is there really much hanky-panky, or even the bare possibility of it, going on in Thélème? Compare with this immobility the intensely real and purposeful activity of Frere Jean a few chapters previously; a parallel instance is provided - and here again I am much indebted to M. Rigolot[16] - in the Prologue to the **Tiers Livre**, where the piled-up, self-stultifying pluralities of the Corinthian **cohue** contrast sharply with the apparently pointless yet dynamic and meaningful activity of the single individual Diogenes, **n'étant par les magistratz employé à chose aulcune faire: praxis** and **poesis, otium** and **negotium** personified, a parable showing us, as the Prologue to **Gargantua** itself shows us, both the meaning of the book and how we are to understand it: **tolle, lege.**

The **actes et gestes gelés voire constipés** of the Thélémites, and the total absence of time-pieces in this abbey, **ny horologe ny quadrant aulcun,** present us with the prospect which confronts and appals the ardent lover in Marvell's poem **To his coy Mistress**

> And yonder all before us lye
> Desarts of vast Eternity

the everlastingness of the grave where there is no device and no embracing; and the only way of raising those Thélémites into some semblance of paradoxical life is, I suggest, to see them as figures in a rich and opulent tapestry.

FAY CE QUE VOULDRAS, then, so far from being the splendid standard-bearer of a lithe and emancipated individuality, and whatever philosophical or metaphysical gloss we may care to put upon the word **THELEMA,** looks more like the swimmer in Stevie Smith's poem 'not waving but drowning'. Thélème is built, as that same RIGOLOT explains, and indeed as Rabelais tells us himself **en toutes lettres,** for the artist's deepest sense is literal, and aesthetic surface gives access to all the depths that human beings can ever know, really know, in the way in which Adam knew Eve his wife, and in

which Job says 'I know that my Redeemer liveth', Thélème is built
upon an enigma, a contradiction in terms; for GOD, being a spirit,
is not worshipped in a temple made with hands, that's for sure, even
if it is **cent foys plus magnificque que n'est Bonivet ne Chambourg
ne Chantilly**; and, as Hugh Kingsmill reminds us, those who seek the
Kingdom alone will find it together, and those who seek it in
company will perish by themselves.

That is why, at the end, Rabelais seals off this 'ballon
d'essai' from real life, since, while Frere Jean may have wanted it,
and while Gargantua may have planned it, it is Rabelais/Alcofribas/
Prospero who is really in charge throughout, and who sees that this
anti-couvent, this **contr'abbaye** has as little to do with the world
outside as that **abbaye** or **couvent** of which it is given as the formal
and explicit antithesis, **les extrêmes**, as Pascal tells us, **se
joignant** – he seals it off in and by the palpably fairy-tale **autant
se entreaymoient ilz à la fin de leurs jours comme le premier de
leurs nopces**; and it is worth noting here that, after Gargantua's
initial **chiquenaude**, his **fiat Thelema, Ainsi l'avoit** estably
Gargantua, pluperfect tense, he, like Frere Jean, plays no further
part in this dumb-show; they do not make up the number of the
Thélémites to 9334, any more, come to that, than do those **qui le
sainct Evangile/En sens agile** [annoncent], and whose invitation to
come in is confined strictly to the **Inscription mise sus la grande
porte** – or, if they do come in, they don't do so as **prescheurs
evangelicques** but as moppers and mowers and tuggers of the
collective forelock like all the others. And so Rabelais adds 'in
case any of you may be thinking that anyone can live in Thélème for
ever – even the Thélémites themselves don't do that', he adds, in
the order of imagination which is the order of his writing and
therefore of our reading, and in a great if equally palpable shaft
of studied nonchalance, of contrived and deliberate clumsiness, and
in the manner of an auld sweetiewife saying 'silly old me, fancy me
almost forgetting to tell you this', **Je ne veulx oublier vous
descripre un enigme**, he says, **qui feut trouvé au fondemens de
l'abbaye.** 'Don't stay too long, **mes enfants**, with that little
carousel, it is only alas! the baseless fabric of my vision of a
prelapsarian Eden, and not of this harsh world the place where, in
the end, we find our happiness, or not at all'. Before one stone is
placed upon another, with his **grande lame de bronze** he saps and
undermines Thélème in its very foundations, only, being Rabelais,
the biggest joker in the pack, he does so a **posteriori**, now you see
it now you don't, it disappears like snow off a dyke or **tenuis ceu
fumus in auras** 'like smoke in thin air'. And, with Saint Paul
saying at the end of I Corinthians chapter 12 'Yet show I unto you a

more excellent way', he debouches, and we must debouch with him, we must follow this auld sweetiewife with sheepish sequacity, he debouches on to the real terrain of the Enigma, which he gives to be solved, all the others having gone to their reward at the end of the war, by the only two real individuals left in the book. This eruption, on to the **tréteaux** of the last page, of Gargantua and Frere Jean, is both a dramatic and a thematic necessity, but thematic because dramatic, not the other way about; and it is hard to think of anything in all Rabelais which has been more cunningly sited than this shutter-and-opener of a sentence, this perfect Janus a-glitter with denotations and connotations too numerous to mention. It is a master-stroke which fills me, for one, **mais que chacun abonde en son sens**, with awe, terror and delight.[17]

In the economy of the last seven chapters, and in the structure of the book as a whole, Thélème is a **leurre**, a **piège**, a trap set for the unwary, **ignis maxime fatuus**, a dangerous testing-ground over which we are made to pass like Tamino and Pamina in the **Magic Flute**. Even from the very gates of Heaven, says John Bunyan, there is a way which goes straight down to Hell. Thélème is, I believe, Rabelais's way down to Hell. I have tried to articulate the dismay, darkness and horror which fall upon me and on everyone, I believe, who negotiates with an equal mind these difficult chapters, so much more puzzling and enigmatic than the Enigma itself or than either of its solutions. But I am certain, from evidence both 'internal' and 'external' - and about these little charmers, stacked cards and loaded dice there is a large and liberating book requiring to be written, for, of the pair of them **internal/external, Oedipus/Schmoedipus**, which is the justice, and which is the thief?[18] - I am certain that not one syllable of these chapters has been written, or altered, under the pressure of events, since whatever they mean and however we may interpret them (and anybody can shoot my interpretation down in flames, **je ne demande pas mieux**) they are part and integral parcel of **Gargantua**'s commanding form, and were allowed by Rabelais himself to be so for the last eighteen years of his life, side by side with those entire and perfect chrysolites the **Prologue**, the **Propos des Bien Ívres**, the stupendous metaphor of the bells, the **chapitre des torcheculs** that cleanser of the doors of our perception and spiritual arse-wiper **hors concours et hors série**, the **querelle des fouaciers et des bergers**, the great helter-skelter of the **chapitre des gouverneurs de Picrochole**, (je dis bien **Picrochole**, crachons, en passant, sur Gaucher de Sainte-Marthe, sur Noël Béda, et, passant un peu plus outre, sur le saint Empereur romain lui-même Charles-Quint),[19] the harangue of Ulrich Gallet, and the defence of Seuilly. The poet whom we set shoulder to shoulder with Shakespeare and Cervantes does not write under the pressure of events, and he is not to be explained by them: that is the easy way out, **facilis descensus Averno** etc., but it is a sterile **impasse** and a **voie sans issue; et l'âme de Rabelais, comme celle de Molière, est d'une grande sérénité**, the serenity of the unmoved mover, the Father of lights, with whom is no variableness neither shadow of turning; and Art is a cold, cold climate.

When we come to Frere Jean's reading of the Enigma, his words are by no means bombinating in a vacuum, which the work of art, being a **plenum** like nature itself, notoriously abhors, since, by the end of the book, by the principle of artistic torque or accumulated import, he has built up with us a huge **crédit** of goodwill. He has been on the right side in the war, he has saved Seuilly, his **baston de la croix** dominates all this part of the book, and being high and lifted up it draws all readers to its Samsonian splendour. He has been true to the **Evangile** in his remark that **les heures sont faictez pour l'homme et non l'homme pour les heures.** He has been the life and soul of every party which he has graced with his exuberant presence. Above all he has taken part, in chapter 38, in a dialogue with Gargantua which is shot through and through with the spirit, and reproduces in places the very verbal movement and dramatic confrontation, of Matthew chapter 25. **Chascun le soubhayte en sa compaignie,** says Gargantua. **Il n'est poinct bigot, il n'est point dessiré** [i.e. he's all of a piece, **il marche tout entier vers sa croissance et sa décroissance**], **il est honeste, joyeulx, deliberé, bon compaignon. Il travaille; il labeure, il defend les opprimez; il conforte les affligez; il souvient es souffreteux; il garde le clous de l'abbaye.** And Jean deflects and disclaims such christocentric compliments, removing all possible embarrassment to any or all of the **assistans**, in one of the most wonderful, one of the noblest passages in all literature, **et qui passe tout commentaire**

> Cedite Romani scriptores cedite Graii,
> Nescio quid maius nascitur Iliade.
> 'Give way, writers of Greece, writers of Rome;
> something greater even than the **Iliad** is born'.

Je foys (dist le Moyne) bien dadventaige;   car, en despeschant noz matines et anniversaires on cueur, ensemble je fois des chordes d'arbaleste, je polys des matraz et guarrotz, je foys des retz et des poches à prendre les connins. Jamais je ne suis oisif. Mais or czà, à boyre, boyre czà . . . The whole speech is a **cocasse** and apparently trivialising send-up, but a send-up in the very spirit of those who in Matthew 25 say - and of course we have to alter the pronouns - **Lord, when saw we thee an hungred and fed thee? or thirsty and gave thee drink? When saw we thee a stranger and took thee in? or naked and clothed thee? or when saw we thee sick and in prison, and came unto thee?**

I suggest therefore that Frere Jean's solution is simply an allegorical transposition of the Enigma in the spirit of the New Testament, as Gargantua's solution is in the spirit and in the letter of the Old. The catastrophes in the poem which, in one of its less enigmatic modes, that of the **monde à l'envers**, has much in common with D'Aubigné's **Tragiques** of which it seems to be a prophetic **raccourci**, and also with the great speech of Ulysses, on degree, in **Troilus and Cressida**:

> Take but degree away, untune that string,
> And hark! What discord follows!

the fire, flood and earthquake, the strife of father against son, friends and relations at each other's throats, those who should be last being first and vice-versa - all these things, all this **tintamarre et brouillamini**, are described as happening imminently

> cest hyver prochain, sans plus attendre
> Voyre plus tost en ce lieu où nous sommes

in and to this transitory, sublunary, extra-Thelemitic world of time and chance, crammed full of **horologes** and **quadrants**. Frere Jean translates these horrors into the different bits and pieces and performers in a game of tennis. He belongs, as his creator belongs, to **un siècle qui veut croire**, and it is not, I think, being too fanciful to suppose that somewhere in the middle of his quasi-analphabetic skull he still retains - or perhaps Rabelais will retain it on his behalf, the creator will do this little thing for his creature in whom he is well pleased? - he still retains some dim and sub-fusc memory of the words of St John's Gospel, chapter 16, verse 33 and last, uttered by another so-called gluttonous man and wine-bibber: **These things I have spoken unto you, that in me ye might have peace. In the world ye shall have tribulation, but be of good cheer: I have overcome the world.**

Since then this is the very best of good news, **l'Evangile au suprême degré**, what more appropriate attitude can Frere Jean possibly adopt towards it, to show his **contemptus huiusce mundi**, than to treat this world as just a game of tennis, et il ferait trop d'honneur à son sujet, n'est-ce pas, s'il le traitait de façon plus

respectueuse? His triviality is suffused and permeated by the **Evangile,** the evangelism of his reading is in direct proportion to its triviality, and goes **pari passu** with it; and his interpretation, therefore, so far from contradicting Gargantua's, or being in any way at variance with it, confirms in fact and complements it. That is why they are on the same see-saw, why they are both performing, as Dorothy Coleman points out with that critical sagacity which we all expect from her, and not in vain, on every page she writes, they are both performing a linguistic dance.[20] 'All the world's a stage', says Jacques in **As You Like it,** 'and all the men and women merely players'. Macbeth says

> Life's but a walking shadow, a poor player
> That struts and frets his hour upon the stage,
> And then is heard no more;

and Lear says, with even more caliginous gloom

> When we are born, we cry that we are come
> To this great stage of fools.

These images are fully understood only in their dramatic contexts; but even out of context their nearness to, and, more importantly, their great distance from Frere Jean's comparison, are clearly apparent.

His reading therefore provides us, at the very end of the book, and in Edition A, with a little **boîte à Silène** whose **enseigne exterieure** seems to have been fashioned **en guaieté de cueur** and designed merely to **exciter le monde à rire,** but which, in its dramatic context, obliges us to revise sharply upwards our first estimate of it as not being worth a **coupeau d'oignon,** and to interpret it **à plus hault sens et en la perfectissime partie.** For just as Rabelais, like the **Pauvre Villon** of David Kuhn's phrase, is in his own way and **mutatis mutandis** of course, a **Christ burlesque**[21] - and that remark by itself is worth every **centime** of the unconscionable price demanded for Kuhn's book by the **Librairie Armand Colin** - so Frere Jean is a burlesque **miles Christianus,** but a **miles Christianus en sens agile** nonetheless. At the very height of the storm, and in that Kingdom which is within, he is, like Saint Paul, at peace, active and unafraid, and he has that in him which Panurge would fain call master.[22] He has nothing but scorn for the **fuyars de Pavye,** and in Gethsemane he would have rushed to defend Jesus **en couppant les jarretz à Messieurs les Apostres,**[23] such a mistake, such a **culpa** but surely **felicissima, quae talem atque**

29

tantum servare cupiisset Redemptorem? for has he not chosen that good part which shall not be taken away from him? He loves the good things of this life, of course he does, not being an eejit, but he's never too drunk or too bloated to **défendre les opprimés, conforter les affligés, ou garder le clos de l'abbaye,** for he knows that these good things are his only in usufruct, not in possession, and taking no thought for the morrow, what he will eat or what he will drink, he is ready at any or every moment of his life to say with the Ronsard of the **Derniers Vers**

> Il faut laisser maisons et Vergers et jardins
> Vaisselles et vaisseaux que l'artisan burine
> Et chanter son obseque en la façon du Cygne
> Qui chante son trépas sur les bors Maeandrins.

Frere Jean is a great and grotesque exemplar, a lad unparalleled, he is not an object of satire; or, if he **is** an object of satire, it is in such a way that with his stripes we may be healed. **Omne enim tulit punctum Rabelaesus qui miscuit utile dulci;** and can we seriously doubt that, at the end of the day, this Israelite indeed in whom is no guile will be urged at that banquet **où lui et les autres joueurs du jeu de paume, après avoir bien travaillé, s'en sont allés repaître,** 'Friend, go up higher; thou hast been faithful over a few things, I will make thee ruler over many things; enter thou into the joy of thy lord'?

I'd like finally to say something about the profound re-working of Frere Jean's words as they appear in Edition E. In the first place, and most obviously, there is a great increase in the number of points of contact between the world of the Enigma and the game of tennis. The perfectly adequate, yet somewhat skeletal correspond- ences of the first edition are now more fully fleshed out, and this multiplication of the trivial details, enhancing as they do the evangelical tenor of the words, underlines Jean's chuckling contempt for this passing show and battered caravanserai; since, the more numerous and the more inconsequential they, the more evangelical he, **et Rabelais le fait savoir à qui le veut entendre.** Next, this Christian buffoon is now clearly addressing a much wider audience, and he is aware of himself as speaking **ex cathedra, urbi et orbi,** the bland and innocuous **assistans** now expanding, a great blank- cheque, to include **multitudes, multitudes in the valley of decision.** For his language becomes a good deal more pretentious, there's a good deal more of the **I am Sir Oracle** about it. Immediately after the opening imprecation **Par sainct Goderan!** which, with the closing **et grand chiere!** is the only element to be carried over in identical shape from first edition to last, the bald **Je pense** of Edition A is replaced by **Telle n'est mon exposition**, grandiloquent word, **formule suffisante voire outrecuidante et 'damn-your-eyes'**. He then adds, entirely in the know-all, **je m'en vais parler de toutes choses** manner of Alcofribas himself **Le stille** (i.e. of the Enigma) **est de Merlin le Prophéte**, carefully distinguishing, like some fastidious don, between that expression and the expression **L'Enigme lui-même est de Merlin le Prophéte**; and firmly refusing, like some scrupulous and reverential don, a Bentley, a Housman, a Lachmann or a Scaliger come to judgment, to substitute the meaningless, **impertinent**, preposterous and idiotic **Mellin de Saint-Gelois** for the altogether meaningful, decorous, and beautiful **Merlin le Prophete, la parole de Rabelais**. What in the world happened to Occam's razor? Et que diable **Mellin de Saint-Gelois** vient-il faire dans cette galère? **Solitudinem faciunt, eruditionem appellant.** They make a wilderness, and they call it learning.[24] Then, fortified by such legendary authority, which has about it all the dim yet august grandeur of **Haremburgis qui tint le Maine**, together with the trifling advantage that it actually makes sense, would you believe? of every single one of Rabelais's contexts, far as well as near, for **Gargantua**, depend upon it, like **Pantagruel**, like the **Tiers Livre** and the **Quart Livre**, is nothing, but nothing, if it is not a book in the prophetic mode, agreeably to the double definition of the Latin word **vates**, he proceeds scornfully and comprehensively to dismiss all readings which differ from his own: **Donnez y allegories et intelligences tant graves que voudrez**, he says, **et y ravassez, vous et tout le monde, ainsi que vouldrez.** Professor Screech says that Frere Jean, in his 'amiable theological crassness', is here being inconsistent since he allegorises the Enigma while condemning allegorisation.[25] What Frere Jean condemns, however, is not all allegory, allegory as such, but only **allegories tant graves que vouldrez, allegories à la Frere Lubin**, as any fool can see, but may be it takes a fool to see it; he has no objection whatever to an **allegorie des plus frivoles**, which at this point is just what the doctor ordered. And so this **magister** this **fort en thème** continues with imperturbable assurance **De ma part je n'y pense aultre chose enclous**, he says, **qu'une description du jeu de paulme soubz obscures paroles.**

Now if Rabelais is thus establishing a second network of correspondences, this time between Frere Jean's words and the Prologue to this book, **cela crève les yeux**, they are the **ocliferia** of Seneca, things which strike the eyeballs, and a good many of them, I am delighted to see, have struck Ian Morrison's eyeballs,[26] and those also, I have no doubt, of many many others besides who have no memorial, **les bonnes choses n'étant point inaccessibles en dépit de la Sorbonne et de certaine librairie suisse,** this can only be, can it not? because Rabelais wishes to direct our attention to the person who dominates that Prologue, the figure of Socrates, whose benevolent, magnanimous, self-abnegating spirit informs not only this book, but the **Tiers Livre** and the **Quart Livre** as well; for, if he is not, so to say, the spiritual wing of the Rabelaisian Muse, Socrates is at least one of the brightest of all her feathers, **lucida tela diei,** 'the bright shafts of day' (Lucretius, **De rerum natura** i.147).

The greatly expanded and transformed **mot de l'énigme** is, I suggest to you in all seriousness, a double **boîte à Silène,** with Frere Jean appearing this time in the guise of a burlesque Socrates. After all, since the greater includes the less, if he can be a comical **imitatio Christi** and get triumphantly away with it, why can he not also be a comical **imitatio Socratis?** proceeding, as both he and Socrates do, from the fructifying **cerveau caseiforme** of the 'onlie begetter' himself François Rabelais/Alcofribas Nasier, of whom they are but broken lights and who is much much more than they?

Spiritus intus alit, totamque infusa per artus
Mens agitat molem et magno se corpore miscet.[27]

'An indwelling spirit sustains, and mind, as it courses through the limbs, sways the whole mass, and mingles with the mighty frame'.

All the really significant qualities of the Greek philosopher, with the sole exception of his great learning, may be predicated also of Frere Jean: on the outside, **tousjours riant, tousjours beuvant d'autant à un chascun, tousjours se guabelant,** the life and soul of the party, even their noses are singled out **et mis en vedette;** and, on the inside, these moral and spiritual gifts which they share: **entendement plus que humain, vertus merveilleuse, divin sçavoir, couraige invincible, contentement certain, asseurance parfaicte, desprisement incroyable de tout ce pourquoy les humains tant veiglent, courent, travaillent, navigent et bataillent;** each of them in his own unique way, the incarnation and quintessence of that **Pantagruélisme,** that **certaine gayeté d'esprit conficte en mespris des choses fortuites,**[28] of which, we are assured on the fly-leaf, this book is full to overflowing, and for which, at the very end, this world as a game of tennis provides a perfect, and, I would say, a sublime metaphor. For, if it was needed in Rabelais's time, how much more is it needed now, in the time of $E = mc^2$, the time of the breaking of nations

It is the very error of the moon;
She comes more nearer earth than she was wont,
And makes men mad.

The Christ-like qualities of Socrates are merely proleptic, but Jean having been born, not of the flesh of course but of the word, under the new dispensation, the expressions **divin sçavoir, celeste . . . drogue, entendement plus que humain, vertus merveilleuse,** are all of them to be understood in his case **strictissimo sensu,** if, here and there, with affectionate and synergistic irony: 'he hasn't got much **sçavoir,** poor chap, and very little by way of **entendement,** but such as they are, they are **plus que humains,** they are **divins',** since their source and their guarantor is Jesus himself, **le decours et maintien de verité divine, via veritas vita, tout ce que sommes, tout ce que vivons, tout ce que avons, tout ce que esperons.** So he doesn't possess a single scrap of Socrates' vast learning or wisdom?[29] Was learning or wisdom demanded of any of the twelve disciples, with or without their **jarrets coupés?** and was any great inspection made of their **curriculum vitae** before they were given the command 'Follow me'? **Rien n'est, sinon Dieu, perfaict.** John's strong toil of grace is not in book-learning, but in being and in believing, a belief which issues, **more iureque Aristotelico,** in instant action, **Johannes agonistes, Hercule chrétien;** not that light, but sent widdershins and anfractuously by Alcofribas, to bear witness of that light. And does not Pascal tell us, in a **Pensée** of utmost charity, that people whose faith is not by **connaissance** but by **sentiment du coeur** are **bienheureux et bien légitimement persuadés, et qu'il y a loin de la connaissance de Dieu à l'aimer!**[30] **Beuveurs tresillustres, et vous, Verolés tresprecieux, car à vous, non à aultres, sont dediez mes escriptz** - I say again, **car à vous, non à aultres, sont dediez mes escriptz,** which, when you come to think of it, is Rabelais's way of saying 'I come not to call the righteous, **les doctes, les érudits, les suffisants, les sophistes, les agelastes, les Héraclites, les Sorbonicoles,** but sinners to repentance; car, **doctes et érudits tant qu'on voudra, mais d'abord et surtout il faut être toujours Beuveurs,** toujours **Verolés',** if we wish to understand Rabelais, to make him ours, and to prevent him from being a mighty poet, in his misery, dead. 'Now that my ladder's gone', says Yeats

I must lie down where all the ladders start
In the foul rag-and-bone shop of the heart;

or, as Baudelaire puts it, somewhat less hysterically, having made

33

the discovery that his ladders too were all of them snakes, 'I escaped from all my systems, **et je suis revenu chercher un asile,** he says, **dans l'impeccable naïveté'**;[31] or again, as Horace teaches us, with even bleaker sanity but his promise is secure

quod petis hic est
est Ulubris animus si te non deficit aequus,[32]

Ulubrae being a **petit trou** sunk in the depths of the Pontine marshes, and **aequus animus** being more or less untranslatable, and felt only in the deep heart's core.

In the re-working of these last words in Edition E, **la dernière revue et corrigée par l'auteur,** in this perfect fusion of Prologue and Epilogue, that poetic union in which things can be both separate and welded together in the comeliness and symbiosis of art - **mes fantasies se suyvent,** says Montaigne, **mais parfois c'est de loing, et se reguardent, mais d'une veue oblique**[33] - in this cheerful, laughing benediction and **ataraxia** at both ends of the book, all shall be well, and all shall be well, and all manner of thing shall be well, I see a great example here of the creative error of one artist taking the measure of the terrifying truth of another

mediocribus esse poetis
non homines non di non concessere columnae[34]

'it is not permitted to poets to be just middling, neither by men, nor by gods, nor yet by Messrs Grant and Cutler Ltd., Booksellers, 11 Buckingham Street, Strand, London WC2N 6DQ'. Thank you for bearing with me this far, **et grand chiere!**[35]

George Sutherland   University of Glasgow

NOTES

1. All quotations from **Gargantua** are from the T.L.F. edition (ed. M.A. Screech), Genève, Droz, 1970.

2. Virgil, **Aeneid** ii, line 1.

3. See E. Cassirer, **Philosophy of Symbolic Forms** (1923-31), trans. R. Manheim, 3 vols., New Haven, 1953-57, condensed into his **Essay on Man,** New Haven, 1944. But by far the most useful of

all his pages, for those whose concern is with literary criticism, are those on 'The problem of form and the problem of causality', in **The Logic of the Humanities**, New Haven, 1961.

4. This has been the thesis since 1956 of Professor M.A. Screech, in several articles of which these are the most important:
   (i) **Bibliothèque d'Humanisme et Renaissance**, XVIII, 1956 pp.392-404: 'The Sense of Rabelais's **Enigme en Prophétie** (Gargantua LVIII): A Clue to Rabelais's Evangelical Reactions to the Persecution of 1534.
   (ii) **Etudes rabelaisiennes** VIII, 1969, pp.109-14: 'Some Reflexions on the Abbey of Thelema'.
   (iii) **Etudes rabelaisiennes**, XI, 1974, pp.9-56: 'Reflexions on the Problem of dating **Gargantua** (A + B)'.
   (iv) **Etudes rabelaisiennes**, XIII, 1976, pp.79-111: 'Some further Reflexions on the Dating of **Gargantua**'.
   Professor Screech's book **Rabelais**, Duckworth, 1979, deals with the question on similar lines, pp.195-206 - The thesis has won the support not merely of scholars in the traditional mould like Jean Larmat, in his 'Le Moyen Age dans le 'Gargantua' de Rabelais', Les Belles Lettres, 1973, p.246, but also of F. Rigolot in his excellent, pragmatically-based book on **Les Langages de Rabelais, Etudes rabelaisiennes**, X, 1972: 'Gargantua, qui incarne les préoccupations des humanistes de 1534, avant l'Affaire des Placards, jette sur le poème le regard même de ses inquiétudes . . . Le géant a pour lui la vérité **historique**, la situation tragique des Evangéliques' (p.98).

5. (i) Oeuvres de François Rabelais, éd. critique publ. par Abel Lefranc . . . t.II, **Gargantua** XXIII-LVIII, P. Champion, 1913.
   (ii) **Gargantua** éd. J. Plattard (**Les Belles Lettres**), 3e ed., 1946.
   (iii) Oeuvres, éd. P. Jourda, Paris, Garnier, Vol. I, 1962.
   (iv) **Gargantua**, éd. M.A. Screech, T.L.F., Genève, Droz, 1970.

6. M.A. Screech in B.H.R. 1956, art. cit. p.392 'The problem of the Enigma has recently been studied by Professor E.V. Telle in a scholarly article [François Rabelais, 4e centenaire de sa mort 1953: E.V. Telle, 'Thélème et le Paulinisme matrimonial érasmien,' pp.104-19, esp. pp.114ff.] His argument that it is Gargantua's interpretation that is to be taken seriously, and not Friar John's, will surely win general approval'.

7. **Tiers Livre**, éd. Jourda, t.I, p.483.

8. James Joyce, **A portrait of the artist as a young man** [1916], ed. Richard Ellmann (London, 1968), p.219.

9. Petronius Arbiter, **Satirae**, 118, 5.

10. Virgil, **Eclogues**, iv, line 1.

11. Ronsard, **Sonnets pour Hélène**, Second Livre, LXXV, lines 3-4 (**Oeuvres complètes**, Pléiade, éd. G. Cohen, t.I, p.277).

12. Walter de la Mare, **Miss T.**, lines 1-4.

13. F. Rigolot, op. cit., pp.77-98.

14. **Gargantua** (T.L.F.), p.301.

15. **Gargantua** (T.L.F.), pp.302-3.

16. F. Rigolot, op. cit., pp.99-102.

17. Professor Screech, commenting on the sentence **Je ne veulx oublier vous descripre un enigme** [E.R. VIII, 1969, art. cit. p.112], after citing **d'autant se entraymoient ilz à la fin de leurs jours comme le premier de leurs nopces**, asks 'Did ever a major author more crudely stick another bit on the end?'

18. 'External' tends to be equated with 'objective, sure, reliable', 'internal' with 'subjective, impressionistic, **sujet à caution**'. But it is belief in the former which has given us all those **Evangéliques** of whom not one is to be found in **Gargantua**, as it has given us Noël Béda, Gaucher de Saint-Marthe, Charles-Quint, and Mellin de Saint Gelais, whom only the eye of faith can see there.

19. Picrochole is derived from πικρόχολος , 'homme qui abonde en bile amère': that is certain. Equally, his henchmen Merdaille and Bas de Fesses are cognate with **merde** and **fesses** respectively: that, too, is certain. If we identify Picrochole with Charles-Quint, why stop there? Why not identify Merdaille and Bas de Fesses with correlatives in 'real' life'? Forty years ago the New Variorum edition of Shakespeare's **Sonnets** (t.II 1944, ed. E. Hyder Rollins) exposed with

merciless comicality the folly of all such identifying ploys: 'the total lack of evidence to support an identification of the woman, or women, of the Sonnets has been only a slight deterrent. She is (or they are) with confidence given a local habitation and a name, irrespective of whether she be a negro prostitute, a Stratford girl or matron, an unchaste maid of honour, an innkeeper's wife of loose morals, a countess or a queen. The glib fashion in which the reputation of the Virgin Queen and other estimable ladies is besmirched should give one pause for meditation' (p.255). But

> The further off from England
> The nearer is to France.

20. D.G. Coleman, **Rabelais: A Critical Study in Prose Fiction**, Cambridge, 1971, p.180.

21. D. Kuhn, **La Poétique de François Villon**, Paris, A. Colin, 1967, p.458.

22. **Quart Livre**, (éd. Jourda), t.II, Chapters XVIII-XXIII.

23. **Gargantua** (T.L.F.), p.224.

24. The **Edition critique**, t.II, p.437, while attributing authorship of the Enigma to Mellin de Saint-Gelais, goes on at once to say 'Le surnom de **prophète** est en rapport avec le caractère de cette énigme "en prophetie". Il évoque le souvenir de Merlin, l'enchanteur des romans bretons . . .'; and again I ask, what happened to Occam's razor? Why scatter darkness upon light? Is this not an example of gratuitous obfuscation?

25. M.A. Screech, **Rabelais**, Duckworth, 1979, p.198.

26. Ian R. Morrison, 'Ambiguity, Detachment and Joy in **Gargantua**', **M.L.R.** 1976, pp.513-22.

27. Virgil, **Aeneid** vi, lines 726-7.

28. **Quart Livre**, éd. Jourda, t.II, **Prologue**, pp.11-12.

29. He does of course possess such a scrap, whose Socratic origin Professor Screech was the first to point out [**Etudes rabelaisiennes**, VIII, 1969, 'Some Reflexions on the Abbey of Thelema', p.111] 'Car comment (disoyt il) pourroys je gouverner

aultruy, qui moymesmes gouverner ne sçauroys?' (T.L.F. ed. p.280). But (a) this is a piece of folk-wisdom which might fall from the lips of anybody with a modicum of self-knowledge. (b) it is much more securely tethered to the Socrates of the **Prologue** than, as Professor Screech suggests, to the Socratic inspiration of the Abbaye de Thélème, since this similarity-in-difference suffuses the whole book, and not merely a few chapters at the end.

30. Pascal, **Pensées,** éd. M. Le Guern (Folio 1977) t.I, fragments 101 and 367.

31. Baudelaire, **Curiosités esthétiques,** ed. Jean Adhémar (Editions de l'Oeil), 1956, p.200.

32. Horace, **Epistles** I,xi, lines 29-30.

33. Montaigne, (Pléiade 1950), III,9, p.1115.

34. Horace, **Ars Poetica,** lines 372-3.

35. This paper has attempted to place the last page of **Gargantua** where alone it belongs i.e. with all the others. It is, however, by no means the only passage whose clear and plain meaning has been distorted by the almost exclusively centrifugal treatment given to this book by historically-minded critics; other examples are the great metaphor of the bells (chapter XVI-XIX), the harangue of Ulrich Gallet (chapter XXIX), and, of course, the entirety of the **guerre picrocholine.**

LANGUAGE IN THE 'TIERS LIVRE'

Dorothy Gabe Coleman

I am not concerned with Rabelais's motives nor his intentions as they can only be hazarded, hypothetically. I am concerned with the text in the form in which he left it. And the text is a fiction. Its texture is tough, ambiguous and rich and it is, as Dr Terence Cave has recently shown us, heavily tied to the whole question of writing in the French Renaissance.[1] The plurality of verbal surfaces forces the critic to meditate and that is the value of all good literature. Of his four authentic works, it is the **Tiers Livre** which taxes the reader in an exciting and yet disturbing way. We find that we must be exceptionally alert readers before we can 'sniff' the text at all and it does force the reader to ask the question of 'How to read a page of Rabelais?'

It is Rabelais's use of language to obtain a total, complex, emotional response that is essential. Yet the bulk of Rabelaisian scholarship is concerned with his 'philosophy', his religion, his legal and medical authority, his humanism and his Christian-Stoic wisdom rather than with the words on the page. The **Tiers Livre** in particular seems to be a work where the detective interest supersedes the critical. Naturally, only the words of the **Tiers Livre** are the **full, total** statement or description. But what the critic can do is to help, in Eliot's words, 'the return to the work of art with improved perception and intensified, because more conscious, enjoyment'.

How many of his own contemporaries understood **Le Tiers Livre**? Certain scholars would say all the élite. I think that it is still an unanswered question. Rabelais is a writer in love with his medium. His inspiration is primarily literary. 'To read attentively, think correctly, omit no relevant consideration, and repress self-will, are no ordinary accomplishments' as A.E. Housman once said and indeed this close reading is the basis of the interpretative process. We must submit to the creative presence; we must determine 'tone-values'; we must realize that comparison and analysis are the chief tools of a critic; and we must realize that close reading is bound to remain creative conjecture.

The aesthetic, procreative corporeality of words and the restorative thrust of writing are among the most pronounced features of Rabelais's work. Knowing 'about' Rabelais and reconstructing the 'social', the 'religious' or the 'moral' context is just not being responsive to the fiction as fiction. The interplay of texts is partly a question of language in all four authentic books. Changes of tone are in many ways the first and the last thing that the reader must heed. In the Prologue to the **Tiers Livre** the roar and clatter are audible; the rapid flow of verbs calls for a perpetual attentiveness on the part of the reader; attempts at elucidation and interpretation are part of the work of the reader and he must be active in this creative partnership with the author; there are no stage-directions.

We can start noticing changes in tone by looking at what Rabelais says about religion. There is a very firm statement about religion expressed through his appreciation of Diogenes as a philosopher,

> en son temps il feut philosophe rare et joyeux entre mille. S'il avoit quelques imperfections, aussi avez vous, aussi avons nous.   Rien n'est, sinon Dieu, perfaict.[2]

He includes in this judgment his intended readers, Diogenes and himself. The tone is clearly serious. Later in the Prologue he makes a comparison between Diogenes rolling his barrel and himself composing his work,

> Icy beuvant je delibere, je discours, je resoulz et concluds. Après l'epilogue je riz, j'escripz, je compose, je boy.

From the convincing tone of the earlier sentence we are now aware here of a light-hearted tone; he revels in the sound of the words, making the two phrases symmetrical, and revealing the way that laughing, writing, composing and drinking are parts of his way of life. He continues in the same tone, sidling into a literary topos: that of wine-drinkers versus water-drinkers in the composition of literature (Classical writers like Horace, Ovid and Propertius had treated the same theme),

> Ennius beuvant escrivoit, escrivant beuvoit.

This quaffing of liquid whilst constructing in words is in the mouth of Ennius here instead of **je**. So also was the way of Aeschylus but as this latter author is more unknown to readers Rabelais puts in brackets '(si à Plutarche foy avez in **Symposiacis**)' a proof or non-proof of the way Aeschylus worked. So too Homer and Cato were people who never wrote till after they had drunk. Rabelais continues 'I don't mind you having a tipple or two either, my dear friends, pourveu que du tout louez Dieu un tantinet'. The phrase **un tantinet** - just a little - is appropriate for Rabelais as a fiction writer **never** commits himself to any religious position, bar the important sentence "Rien n'est, sinon Dieu, perfaict". Scholars push him along a linear path and thereby reduce him in stature and diminish his responsibility as a writer. It is important that we **always** remember this point about his stance in religion and it is important too to notice the serious tone and the light-hearted tone; the two edging each other put in perspective and provide the background to the **Tiers Livre.**

The difference between this passage and the last few sentences in the Prologue is violent. Let me quote the passage in Urquhart's version - since the Colloquium is taking place in Scotland; he is talking about hypocrites,

> Do you jog hither, wagging your Tails, to pant at my Wine, and bepiss my Barrel? Look here is the Cudgel, which Diogenes, in his last Will, ordained to be set by him after his Death, for beating away, crushing the Reins, and breaking the Backs of these Bustuary Hobgoblins, and Cerberian Hell-hounds. Pack you hence therefore, you Hyppocrites, to your Sheep-dogs. Get you gone you Dissemblers, to the Devil. Hey! What, are you there yet? I renounce my part of Papimanie. If I snatch you, Grr, Grrr, Grrrrrr. Avant, Avant! Will you not be gone? May you never shit till you be soundly lash'd with Stirrup-leather, never piss but by the Strapado, nor be otherways warmed, than by the Bastinado.

The passage is tinged with excretory vocabulary: 'bepiss', 'shit' and 'piss'. The violent tone comes through the tortures of the strappado, the thrashing and thwacking, the beating and cudgelling, the crushing of the kidneys and breaking the backs of 'these Bustuary Hobgoblins'. The tone is bawdy, racy, explosive and scatological. It is not meant for the squeamish. The omniscient narrator has the maddened tone of a person wishing to pulverize hypocrites through his verbal diarrhoea. Into this passage comes a note about religion,

Je renonce ma part de Papimanie, si je vous happe . . .

Papimanie - papistry. Popish dotage or a doting on the Pope - is introduced here in a whirlpool of curses, hell-hounds and devils.

It is bound by the context and the difference between a mocking tone and a serious tone can only be measured when we have read and re-read the whole Prologue. In fact the blustery violent tone here with its mixture of exclamations, imperatives and the scowling use of 'Gzz, gzzz, gzzzzzz' - non-words which call up a visualisation and a hearing of an irritated bull-mastiff barking 'bowgh wawgh' at intruders - foretells numerous occasions in the book when Panurge will have the same tone as the omniscient narrator.

There is also a scoffing tone when the narrator mocks lawyers, doctors, hypocrites and critics of his work, calling them

> avalleurs de frimars . . . grabeleurs de correction . . . des caphars . . . ces larves bustuaires et mastins Cerbericques.[3]

Here is the authentic scholar ridiculing scholarship; here is a lawyer who derides law and here is a medical doctor who makes fun of medicine. Rabelais is against the presumption that accompanies learning and erudition, whether it be from the 'good' characters like 'le bon Pantagruel' and 'le bon Gargantua' or from amoral persons like Panurge, Her Trippa, Janotus, Homenaz, Picrochole, Frère Jean, Hippothadée or Rondibilis. Fools have a trust in jargon, in the magic power of the word, in professionalism, in superstition, mystery and **scientia.** Rabelais plays on fools and rogues with fantasy, with poetry and with laughter.

What is the **Tiers Livre** about? Will Panurge be a cuckold if he gets married? I do not know whether he will be married or not; nor does any of his friends in the book. For Panurge never gets married. Superficially, the quest is gratuitous indeed. But, the fiction is partly that of quest and the comic vision goes deep. We know Pantagruel's statement (which thinkers such as Aristotle or Dante had made before) that,

> C'est abus dire que ayons languaige naturel. Les languaiges sont par institutions arbitraires et convenences des peuples.[4]

Communication is arbitrary; speech depends on two people making the effort to understand; words are merely the coins of significance; we change money with each other all the time. Pantagruel and Panurge do not have the right change. They go through a whole book with neither understanding what the other means. Both use rhetoric to prove that black is white and vice-versa. We are in the world of Ionesco or Beckett. But no . . . Rabelais's world is different, for

from the arbitrary nature of communication comes the whole
splendiferous universe, an enormously huge bubble which does not get
pricked. Rabelais is a poet fascinated by the whole phenomenon of
language; the real life that words seem to have, an animated
movement on the confines of articulation. The role of the
imagination in Rabelais is vast. We should not think of him as
sharing the views of the giants but rather as imagining a
contrasting pair of characters - Pantagruel and Panurge. The poetic
play of fancy and the concept of humanity - these are keys to his
comic vision of the world. Rabelais's work stands or falls as
embodying artistic beauty.

Comedy rests on wrong principles with perfectly valid reasons;
the upsetting of the normal outlook with a substitution of the
absurd and then working on that as if it were the normal. Panurge
is the character with the most imagination: he almost stands for
the negation of life and the predominance of words. Yet, he does
have one characteristic which is human,

> les beaulx bastisseurs nouveaulx de pierres mortes ne sont
> escriptz en mon livre de vie. Je ne bastis que pierres
> vives, ce sont hommes.[5]

Meredith, in his subtle essay on comedy, says 'Panurge is comic but
only a Rabelais could set him moving with real animation'. He is a
clever fool in purely linguistic terms as he wanders about a
universe which is full of words. In speaking rhetorically well
about, for instance debts, he delights the reader with his erudite
ingenuity. With Panurge we get the same **sorcellerie évocatoire** as
we get with Her Trippa or Homenaz. Everyone in Pantagruel's company
knows that Panurge is marching in a different way from the
commonsensical norm but everyone is tolerant because he is fun. The
comedy in the **Tiers Livre** is more intellectual than in any of the
other books: it questions among other things the allegorical way of
interpreting events. The omniscient narrator is in control: he
places the two characters in opposite directions around allegory.
The **Tiers Livre** questions human knowledge and is consciously
ambiguous in introducing themes - be they serious, absurd, obscene
or farcical - merely as pretexts.

We may define verbal fantasy as the pleasure that comes from
playing with words not so much for what they mean but from the
intellectual joy of swirling them. Aragon and Apollinaire play on
words in their poetry and the mystery and power of their punning
give us one of the elements at the root of literary excitement -
recognition. In Rabelais too, words call to each other in ebullient

and effervescent ways.   There is a peppy tone, full of punch, guts,
vim and verve.   We see it at the very beginning of the Prologue
where the omniscient narrator is playing with the reader, a 'thrice-
precious Gouty' man who drinks as much as he likes.   In the first
paragraph the theme is 'seeing' - 'veistes vous, si l'avez veu, vous
n'aviez perdu la veue' being tied on to the non-sensical way of
seeing Diogenes.   The throwing away immediately afterwards of the
phrase - 'ou je suis vrayement forissu d'intelligence et de sens
logical' - is a hint of the phrase spoken by the omniscient narrator
on Pantagruel's position in chapter 2 -

>   Aussi eust il esté forissu du Deificque manoir de raison
>   . . .

The narrator likes to play tricks on the reader's imagination: for
instance the next sentence almost forces the reader to suggest
himself a few variations after

>   C'est belle chose veoir la clairté . . .

could it be the clearness of wine, sparkling and glittering?   Or
could it be the flashing and glistening of gold?   After leading the
reader up the garden path through the phrase in brackets '(vin et
escuz)' the narrator gleefully tosses in the real clarity of the
Soleil.   The anecdote which follows - that of the blind man in the
Bible - 'les tressacres bibles' (as recounted in the gospels of
Mark, Luke and Matthew) - ends with 'rien plus ne demanda que
veoir'.   Thus the whole paragraph is completed with the word **veoir.**
    This first paragraph is pun-provoking and heady with the sound
of words so that we are not surprised to find the second almost
entirely composed of tricks;   the narrator juggles with words around
the wine theme.   A pun like 'pour en vin, non en vain' is followed
by a mighty alliteration of s and ph

>   ains plus-que-physicalement philosopher

and this in turn encourages the narrator to chase another pun-
alliteration in

>   pour en lopinant opiner . . .

which is a mish-mash of 'thinking' coupled with a very physical verb
- **lopinant,** cutting into little pieces.   The end

> des substances, couleur, odeur, excellence, eminence,
> propriété, faculté, vertus, effect et dignité du benoist
> et desiré piot.

reminds us of the Prologue to **Gargantua** where the narrator compares
his book to Horace's **Odes,** saying

> Autant en dict un tirelupin de mes livres; mais bren pour
> luy.

Then he rolls his words and lobs out this magnificent sentence,

> L'odeur du vin, ô combien plus est friant, riant, priant,
> plus celeste et delicieux que l'huille.[6]

Gaiety and ebullient creativeness in linguistic formulation are
conditions in the two-way process between the reader and Rabelais's
comic texts.

Panurge and Pantagruel are, of course, parodies of the
traditional epic couple. Both have associations with the devil and
both are comic. Pantagruel's pomposity, his rigidity in coming back
again and again to his 'Christian Stoicism', the inconsistency of
his actions, the pure pedantry of his interpretations and the
unshakable faith in the rightness of himself make him unmistakably
comic. Both characters play a game; they confront each other time
and again with opposite interpretations; and the Olympian author is
playing with both of them. For instance in chapter 2, Pantagruel -
who is about to hold forth in a Stoic way - is introduced to us,

> Je vous ay ja dict et encores rediz que c'estoit le
> meilleur petit et grand bon hommet que oncques ceigneit
> espée.

This resembles the giant of the second book,

> Et Pantagruel prenoit à tout plaisir. Car je ause bien
> dire que c'estoit le meilleur petit bon homme qui fust
> d'ici au bout d'un baston.[7]

The shape of comments to come is revealed in chapter 5: Pantagruel
says,

> Vous me usez icy de belles graphides et diatyposes, et me
> plaisent tresbien: mais . . .

whilst in chapter 6 Panurge says,

Je trouve vostre raison bonne et bien fondée. Mais . . .

This **voyre mais** device is going to be staple diet in the **Tiers Livre**. It is used by both characters. The omniscient narrator gives roughly the same phrase to both. For instance in chapter 9 Panurge 'dist avecques un profond souspir' whilst in chapter 12, it is Pantagruel who 'dist à Panurge en souspirant'. In chapter 12 we hear Pantagruel say,

> Plus vous diray, et le prendrez comme extraict de haulte mythologie . . .

whereas in chapter 18, it is Panurge who says,

> Vous exposez allegoricquement ce lieu et le interpretez à larrecin et furt. Je loue l'exposition, l'allegorie me plaist, mais non à vostre sens.

The search for knowledge is burlesquely played with when Pantagruel advises Panurge to consult the Sibyl,

> Que nuist sçavoir tousjours et tousjours apprendre, feust ce d'un sot, d'un pot, d'une guedoufle, d'une moufle, d'une pantoufle? (chapter 16)

and in chapter 25 we hear from Panurge as he finally gives in to Epistemon as regards consulting Her Trippa the cuckold - 'On ne sçauroit trop apprendre'.

The intertextuality, the interplay of texts revolves around the language in the four authentic works. Rabelais consciously cultivates ambiguity on the semantic, stylistic and syntactic levels. He plays with tone, with ironic levels and with the sound of the spoken word. Every word of the text matters. Take one adverb - **apertement** - and note how many times it comes in. After the parody of the consultation with the Sibyl, Pantagruel finds her message utterly clear,

> La prophetie de la Sibylle **apertement** expose ce que jà nous estoit denoté par les sors Virgilianes . . . [8]

Pantagruel uses any authority to justify his interpretations: for example after Panurge has recounted his dream, his master can easily find the message of cuckoldry,

> Cestuy poinct est **apertement** exposé par Artemidorus, comme
> le diz.[9]

Hippothadée's consultation is a fine burlesque,

> Le bon Dieu nous a faict ce bien qu'il nous les a revelez,
> annoncez, declairez et **apertement** descriptz par les sacres
> bibles.[10]

Panurge's mention of the Ogygian Isles where soothsayers can
apertement predict people's lots is in chapter 24. Her Trippa
speaks of the divination by mirrors,

> Il ne te fauldra poinct de lunettes. Tu la voyras en un
> mirouoir brisgoutant aussi **apertement** que si je te la
> monstrois en la fontaine du temple de Minerva près Patras.[11]

Words call to each other with contexts fore-ordained. For
instance, after the consultation with Triboullet, Pantagruel
considers the fool's gestures,

> En iceulx j'ay noté **mysteres** insignes, et plus tant que je
> souloys ne m'esbahys de ce que les Turcs reverent telz
> folz comme musaphiz et prophetes.[12]

The term **mysteres** recalls to us the '**mysteres** horrificques' of the
Prologue to **Gargantua**. The other more famous phrase - 'la
sustantificque mouelle' - jolts against the 'substantificque
qualité' in Janotus's speech. The 'symboles Pythagoricques' arrow
onto Pantagruel's Pythagorian and favourable interpretation of
Nazdecabre before the latter sneezes to the left and forces
Pantagruel to give a disastrous message,

> Vertus beuf de boys . . . qu'est ce là? Ce n'est à vostre
> adventaige . . . [13]

The reader darts forwards and backwards as Rabelais bombards him
with words: he reads of Pantagruel's use of 'Caballistes et
Massorethz' (p.116), he hears of Frère Jean's words 'par certaine
Caballisticque institution' (p.119) and Panurge's use of 'Massoreth
et Caballistes' (p.167). Every character uses the same method of
arguing with examples: Panurge is jolly hilarious for instance,

Juno seroit elle putain? Car il s'ensuivroyt par la figure dicte Metalepsis . . . (p.112)

And even more Epistemon when he springs into saying,

je seroys d'advis (paradvanture non seroys) . . . (p.173)

In this paper I have not the time to pursue the analysis of the particular arrangements of words or phrases in their contexts so I shall merely concentrate on Panurge's language and behaviour: he is a big blusterer, wordy but without a password; the grease upon his tongue is thick; remember the great swaggering din with which he shouts his pranks among the Turks in **Pantagruel**; the rascally Turks had put him on a spit, all larded with bacon-slices like a rabbit and his pasha was offering his soul to the devils, Grilgoth, Astaroth, Rappallus and Gribouillis,

Seroyent ilz bien gens pour m'emporter aussi? Je suis jà demy rousty. Mes lardons seront cause de mon mal, car ces diables icy sont frians de lardons, comme vous avez l'autorité du philosophe Jamblicque et Murmault en l'Apologie **De bossutis et contrefactis pro Magistros nostros**. Mais je fis le signe de la croix, criant: **Agyos athanatos, ho Theos!** Et nul ne venoit.[14]

In this burlesque situation Panurge can supply the reader with chapter and verse taken from philosophers. We may also remember the episode of Thaumaste who comes to Paris to consult Pantagruel who,

se promenoit par le jardin avecques Panurge, philosophant à la mode des Peripateticques.[15]

We know that the encounter is hilarious with a game of obscene signs played by Panurge and yet Pantagruel is out for,

ne cherchons honeur ny applausement des hommes, mais la **verité seule**. (my emphasis)

In the **Tiers Livre** we find every character's 'position' around truth and allegory. Epistemon, for instance, finds Panurge's interpretation of Raminagrobis's ugly black beasts wrong,

Il ne l'entend (scelon mon jugement) en telle sophisticque et phantasticque allegorie. Il parle absolument et proprement des pusses, punaises, cirons, mousches, culices, et aultres telles bestes.[16]

Her Trippa's consultation is grotesque,

Voulez vous . . . en sçavoir plus amplement la verité par Pyromantie. par Aëromantie, celebrée par Aristophanes en ses **Nuées** . . . [17]

Amidst the vast list of different ways of divining the truth he suggests the very Virgilian and Homeric lots that the two Ps have tried,

Par Cleromantie, comme l'on trouve la febve on guasteau la vigile de l'Epiphanie.

Also he offers 'Par Stichomantie Sibylline' - thus reversing or turning upside down the story. Notice too that every character goes by the mode of 'par l'autorité' or 'j'entend bien' . . . 'vous inferez que . . .'

Pantagruel's attitude to Panurge's dilemma vacillates wildly. At the beginning he advises Panurge to make up his own mind, whereas after the consultation with Triboullet he says,

Il dict que vous estes fol! Et quel fol? Fol enragé, qui sus vos vieulx jours voulez en mariage vous lier et asservir.[18]

In spite of being in chapter 2 a person who 'Jamais ne se tourmentoit, jamais ne se scandalizoit', when Panurge flippantly says in chapter 11 'let's use dice', he very angrily shouts out,

Non . . . Ce sort est abusif, illicite et grandement scandaleux.

And to the written advice of Raminagrobis he says 'Encores n'ay je veu response que plus me plaise'. The offer of friendship between the two characters remains: 'Je vous seray un Achates' (chapter 47) says Panurge as indeed Pantagruel had proposed in the second book,

et vous et moy ferons un nouveau pair d'amitié telle que feut Enée et Achates.[19]

Panurge confides in Frère Jean that,

Je crains que, par quelque longue absence de nostre roy
Pantagruel, auquel force est que je face compaignie, voire
allast il à tous les diables, ma femme me face coqu . . . [20]

this reminds us of his oath in **Pantagruel** (chapter 9) 'protestant
jamais ne vous laisser; et alissiez vous à tous les diables'. He
states openly to Frère Jean,

Voy là le mot peremptoire; car tous ceulx à qui j'en ay
parlé me en menassent, et afferment qu'il me est ainsi
praedestiné des cieulx.

So, Panurge is 'in on' the game too.

It is in Panurge that we see linguistic comedy at its best. In
the **manger son bled en herbe** chapters he mixes the two meanings -
literal and metaphoric - in a comic and poetic way, making the **bled**
into a **sauce verte** with an **intarissable** list of virtues, all the
essential actions in life **et mille autres rares adventaiges**. The
ebullience and speed with which he can toss off one of his **idées
fixes** like 'je me donne à sainct Babolin le bon sainct' or 'Amen,
amen, fiat! fiatur! ad differentiam papae' delights the reader. It
is precisely the way in which he can create humorous incongruity by
the unexpected exploitation of a scene in a nonsensical manner that
marks him. May I suggest that it is mainly Panurge's character that
is the reason why the **Tiers Livre** is readable today. Most laughter
embodies features of child's play and it is in watching Panurge
making faces, obscene gestures, using disguises, repetitions, echoes
and tricks that we are made to laugh. Temperamentally he is a
quick-silver character from the beginning: his first entry on stage
is a linguistic wonder and makes Pantagruel 'fall in love' with him.
The consultation with Hippothadée is a dramatic scene with Panurge
speaking 'en parfonde reverence' and Hippothadée 'respondit en
modestie incroyable'. Panurge's first speech ends on a delightful
simile,

car vous estes tous esleuz, choisiz et triez, chascun
respectivement en son estat, comme beaulx pois sus le
volet.[21]

A rapid dialogue establishes Panurge's right to marry 'car trop
meilleur est soy marier que ardre on feu de concupiscence'. The
quick reaction of Panurge is to thank him for having spoken so well
without 'circumbilivaginer autour du pot'. He invites Hippothadée
to his wedding, which will be very soon, tells him that they'll have

a goose and asks him to lead off the first dance of his bridesmaids. They are on opposite sides and it is useless claiming that Hippothadée is a good theologian and Panurge is wilfully on the wrong tack. He is on top at the end, twisting the ends of his moustache, saying that 'Thank God! the virtuous woman of Solomon is dead',

> Je ne la veid oncques, que je saiche . . . Grand mercy, toutesfoys, mon pere.[22]

Rondibilis starts his dramatic scene with 'Par les ambles de mon mulet'; he carries on for the next few pages on the four ways of quelling lust and comes to the **acte Venerien** as the fifth way only to be pounced on by Panurge with his animated and mirthful energy 'Je vous attendois là . . . et le prens pour moy'. (Cf. **Pantagruel** chapter 26, where the prisoner says that there are 'cent cinquante mille putains, belles comme deesses' . . . and Panurge's reaction - 'Voilà pour moy'.) Panurge finishes the consultation by acting the part of the doctor, preparing a suppository of warm guts for Rondibilis's wife and,

> Je suys tousjours à vostre commendement.
> En poyant, dist Panurge.
> Cela s'entend, respondit Rondibilis.[23]

With the creation of Panurge, Rabelais is a forerunner of Molière: Panurge can prove that black is white in the same way as Diafoirus can; his age at 35 makes him an old Arnolphe and he is a sketch of Scapin. The vigour, the matter of factness, the ebullient, earthy, even coarse language of Molière is unusual in the elegant, civilised and rather refined milieu of Racine, La Rochefoucauld and Bossuet. But although we do not have documentary evidence to prove it surely he learnt much from Rabelais? The **raideur** of Rondibilis when he says,

> Si ma femme se porte mal, j'en vouldrois veoir l'urine . . . toucher le pouls et veoir la disposition du bas ventre ...[24]

is reminiscent of all doctors in Molière rushing around with syringes ready to give an enema if they can. The supple and subtle comic vision is, I think, best seen in the **Tiers Livre**: the sly and humorous relativity of Rabelais; the elusive and ambiguous Rabelais; an artistic vision based on a tolerant attitude to life; the distance, detachment and tranquility plus the **joie de vivre**, effervescence and the linguistic fun. We can say with Hazlitt,

> Rabelais was laughing at the world and enjoying it by turns, and making the world laugh with him . . . at his teeming wit and its own prolific follies.

Dorothy Gabe Coleman   New Hall, Cambridge

NOTES

1. Terence Cave, **The Cornucopian Text. Problems of writing in the French Renaissance**, Oxford, 1979.

2. References are to the M.A. Screech's edition of **Le Tiers Livre**, Genève/Paris, 1964. Here it is p.9.

3   ed. cit. p.21.

4. p.140.

5. p.59.

6. Pierre Jourda, Rabelais, **Oeuvres complètes**, t.1, p.9.

7. **Pantagruel**, chapter 21, Jourda edition, t.1. p.376.

8. Screech edition, p.133.

9. p.110.

10. p.213.

11. p.182.

12. p.305.

13. p.147.

14. Jourda edition, t.1, p.291.

15. ibid. p.313.

LANGUAGE IN THE **TIERS LIVRE**

16. Screech edition, p.160.

17. p.181.

18. p.309.

19. Jourda edition, t.1, p.269.

20. Screech edition, p.197.

21. p.208.

22. p.215.

23. p.241.

24. p.240.

APHORISMO

RVM HIPPOCRA

SECTIONES
SEPTEM,

*

Ex Franc. Rabelaſi
recognitio-
ne.
Quibus ex Ant. Muſæ Commentariis ad-
iecimus & Octauam : & quædam alia,
quæ ſequens indicabit pagella.

VIRTVTE DVCE COMITE FORTVNA

APVD SEB. GRY-
PHIVM LV-
GDVNI,
1543.

PLEADING, DECIDING, AND JUDGING IN RABELAIS

Ian Morrison

This paper is concerned with two sorts of episode: the first
involves petitioning or making representations to an authority,
normally a king;   the second involves forensic scenes.   That
selection of episodes may be slightly arbitrary. However, I hope
that a certain arbitrariness of perspective may be felt acceptable,
if the perspective reveals some relatively unexplored areas of
interest. More specifically, I hope, by adopting this point of
view, to draw attention to three preoccupations appearing in the
certainly authentic novels: the practical importance, or otherwise,
of rhetorical skills;   the capacity, or otherwise, of the human mind
to unravel problems of legality and justice;   and the moral aspect
of litigation and dispute.[1]

Three main episodes feature petitions or representations: in
Gargantua, Janotus de Bragmardo seeks the return of the bells of
Notre-Dame, and Ulrich Gallet makes representations to Picrochole;
in the Prologue to the **Quart Livre**, Couillatris appeals to Jupiter
for the return of his axe.   First, Janotus.   His mission is
entrusted to him, a theologian, despite protests that a member of
the Faculty of Arts would be more suitable, 'que ceste charge mieulx
competoit à un orateur que à un sophiste' (**Gargantua** 17).[2] He is,
however, accompanied by members of that Faculty, disparagingly
described by the text as 'maistres inertes, bien crottez à profit de
mesnaige' (**Gargantua** 18).[3] Their presence matters, because it is
from one of the 'maistres inertes' that Ponocrates learns the object
of the deputation: 'ilz demandoient les cloches leurs estre
rendues' (**Gargantua** 18).[4] When the coming of the delegation is
reported to Gargantua, two decisions are taken, swiftly and
unanimously: first, to return the bells to the competent
authorities; secondly, to do so before Janotus can give his speech,
so that he may not take unwarranted credit for retrieving the bells
(**Gargantua** 18).[5] Thus, in some thirty lines, quite unknown to
Janotus, his impending speech has become otiose.   Its futility is
underlined subsequently.   In mid-speech Janotus declares that he
will be rewarded if he secures the return of the bells: 'Si vous
nous les rendez à ma requeste, je y guaigneray six pans de saulcices
et une bonne paire de chausses' (**Gargantua** 19).[6] After the speech,
Gargantua and his entourage resolve that they will themselves give
Janotus the promised reward, on the grounds that 'il leurs avoit
donné de passetemps et plus faict rire que n'eust Songecreux'

(**Gargantua** 20).[7] In other words, Janotus is rewarded, not because his speech had effected its object, but because it had been clownish. But of course even the clownishness is accidental; Janotus thinks his address a 'belle harangue' (**Gargantua** 19).[8] The reward from Gargantua may therefore be seen as doubly gratuitous, and so as underlining the gratuitousness of Janotus's speech.

What is the significance of this pointless oration by Janotus? The speech serves partly to exhibit the educational inadequacies of theologians, represented by Janotus, 'le plus vieux et suffisant de la Faculté' (**Gargantua** 17).[9] Among its shortcomings, it is, for example, very wordy. By juxtaposition, it contrasts with the swift decision of Gargantua and his associates to return the bells, and even with the performance of the despised 'maistre inerte', who states the point of the mission in one short sentence. However, because the futility of the speech is quite independent of its rhetorical deficiencies - and thus of the features which make it satirical - the satire does not exhaust the significance of Janotus's speech. Its further significance may be apparent when we have considered the performance of Ulrich Gallet as an emissary from Grandgousier to Picrochole.

Initially, Gallet's task is to ask Picrochole 'pourquoy ainsi soubdainement estoit party de son repous et envahy les terres es quelles n'avoit droict quicquonques' (**Gargantua** 28).[10] In fact, this expression covers a two-fold mission. Explicitly, it is to seek an explanation. But, implicitly, it is also to persuade Picrochole to leave. That latter aim is implied by the words, 'les terres es quelles n'avoit droict quicquonques' and confirmed by the demand which Gallet in fact delivers to Picrochole: 'Depars d'icy presentement, et demain pour tout le jour soye retiré en tes terres' (**Gargantua** 31).[11]

How successful is the mission? First, what does it elicit about Picrochole's motives? His sole reply to Gallet's speech is: 'Venez les querir, venez les querir. Ilz ont belle couille et molle. Ilz vous brayeront de la fouace' (**Gargantua** 32).[12] On this basis, Gallet reports that Picrochole is 'hors du sens et delaissé de Dieu' (**Gargantua** 32).[13]. Fundamentally, this may well be an accurate assessment. However, as Grandgousier's reply indicates, he does not find it immediately helpful: 'Voyre mais . . . mon amy, quelle cause pretend il de cest excès?' Only then does Gallet mention the reference to **fouaces** and speculate that Picrochole's **fouaciers** might have been wronged, a speculation which leads to the discovery that there had indeed been an incident involving the **fouaciers.** Thus, the episode which occasioned the invasion is indeed identified in the wake of Gallet's mission, though it must be said that this identification comes about rather indirectly. As for the other object of the mission, to persuade Picrochole to withdraw, that is clearly not achieved. It is fair to say, therefore, that the first mission is relatively unsuccessful. However, it does at least suggest to Grandgousier a new line of approach to Picrochole. Accordingly, Gallet is sent a second time. Now his mission is to offer **ex gratia** payments to Picrochole and to the injured **fouacier** Marquet, and again to press Picrochole to withdraw his troops. This time, the embassy is interpreted as a sign of fear. Toucquedillon advises Picrochole that 'ces rustres ont belle paour' and successfully urges him to persist in his plans for conquest (**Gargantua** 32).[14] Thus, quite contrary to the intentions of Gallet and Grandgousier, the second mission encourages Picrochole to persevere. Considered jointly, the two missions are an unmitigated failure.

At first sight, this cumulative failure is surprising. Gallet himself is described as an 'homme saige et discret' (**Gargantua** 30).[15] His speeches to Picrochole and Toucquedillon, which are the essence of his missions, appear to have notable rhetorical qualities. And if they are as good as they appear to be, then this would lead us to conclude that Gallet fails despite his rhetorical prowess. Since that would be rather an intriguing conclusion, it is indispensable, at this point, to examine these speeches in some detail, in order to determine how good they are. We may begin with the first **harangue**, which makes up all of chapter 31.

This speech is well organised. First, it refers in general to the outrage and distress of those who have suffered betrayal; then it goes on to the particular case of Grandgousier's grief at being betrayed by Picrochole, and explains the peculiar intensity of that grief by reference to the former celebrated stability of the alliance between the two ('Doncques merveille n'est . . . desisté de leurs entreprises').[16] Next Gallet moves the focus of his remarks from Grandgousier to Picrochole. He first speculates on Picrochole's motives ('Quelle furie doncques te esmeut . . . ?').[17] Then, on the assumption that Picrochole must imagine himself to have some cause of grievance against Grandgousier, Gallet proceeds to outline how he ought to have sought redress ('Si quelque tort eust esté par nous faict . . . ').[18] And having argued thus that, even if Picrochole supposed himself aggrieved, his invasion was unjustified, Gallet concludes by demanding due remedy for the invasion, namely that Picrochole should withdraw and pay reparations ('Depars d'icy presentement . . . ').[19] Viewed as a whole, the speech develops coherently and remains strictly relevant.

Considered in detail, the speech shows eloquence, by which I mean controlled handling of complex and ornate structures. The quality may be illustrated briefly by the example of one sentence, which is set out below so as to bring out its structure:

> Si quelque tort eust esté par nous faict en tes subjectz et dommaines, si par nous eust esté porté faveur à tes mal vouluz, si en tes affaires ne te eussions secouru, si par nous ton nom et honneur eust esté blessé,
>   ou, pour mieulx dire,
> si l'esperit calumniateur, tentant à mal te tirer, eust par fallaces especes et phantasmes ludificatoyres mis en ton entendement que envers toy eussions faict choses non dignes de nostre ancienne amitié,
> tu debvois premier enquerir de la verité, puis nous en admonester, et nous eussions tant à ton gré satisfaict que eusse eu occasion de toy contenter. (**Gargantua** 31)[20]

The structure is pellucid. It is a hypothetical sentence made up of three nearly equal blocks of material: the protasis is two blocks of hypotheses articulated one to the other by the expression 'ou, pour mieulx dire'; the apodosis is the third block. The progression of the sentence is no less clear than its overall shape. The first block of hypotheses reflects circumstances which Gallet treats as inconceivable, since that first block is relegated below the horizon by the correction, 'ou, pour mieulx dire', to be replaced by the second block, the hypothesis of demonically inspired delusions, a hypothesis which Gallet takes seriously, since he is to report Picrochole 'hors du sens et delaissé de Dieu' (**Gargantua** 32).[21] Next, the apodosis starts with two principal clauses, comparatively short and precise statements of what Picrochole ought to have done. These statements have a quality of didactic clarity, enshrined for example in the adverbs, 'premier . . . puis . . .'. And, no doubt because of the businesslike tone of the principal clauses, the consecutive clause in which they culminate takes on an incontrovertible air: 'que eusse eu occasion de toy contenter'. Thus, the sentence is limpid in outline and compelling in progression. The fact that these qualities characterize a nine-clause sentence illustrates what I mean by controlled handling of complex structures.

As for ornateness, it is enough to note, as one possible example, the double chiasmus in the first two clauses of the same sentence:

Si	quelque tort	eust esté	par nous	faict	en tes subjectz
					et dommaines

1	2	3	4

3	2	4	1

Si	par nous	eust esté	porté	faveur	à tes mal vouluz

Clearly, elements 1 and 3 are arranged in chiasmus, as are elements
1 and 4. Importantly, this is not mere embellishment. The
variations in word order delay perception of the meaning of the
opening clauses; by contrast, the second and third blocks into
which the sentence has been analysed move forward to their point
more directly; in short, there is an effect of acceleration through
the sentence from the hypotheses which Gallet treats as unreal
towards the conclusion which he urges seriously at the end of the
sentence. This acceleration is part of the process of persuasion.

On the basis of that summary examination, I suggest that
Gallet's first oration has excellent qualities: intellectually, it
is orderly; aesthetically, it is attractive; and it has the
strictly rhetorical quality of persuasiveness, at least for the
detached reader. What of his second speech?

Unlike the first, it is not highly decorative. It is succinct
(about 16 lines), and simple both in style and in syntax. Gallet,
for example, states baldly that his purpose is 'pour vous . . .
ouster toute excuse que ne retournez en nostre premiere alliance'
(**Gargantua** 32).[22] He makes clear that the payment offered is **ex
gratia**, saying of the **fouaces** 'Cinq douzaines en prindrent noz gens;
elles furent très bien payées; nous aymons tant la paix que nous en
rendons cinq charrettes' (**ibid.**). He unequivocally reasserts that
Picrochole's occupation is wrong, pressing him to give up 'ceste
place icy, en laquelle n'avez droict quelconques' (**ibid.**). In
short, the speech is plainly conciliatory; but equally plainly, it
is not defeatist. To the detached reader, therefore, it seems to
have the major quality of clarity, and not at all to warrant
interpretation by Toucquedillon as a mark of fear.

If Gallet's representations are unsuccessful, it is not because
they are untimely (as in the case of Janotus) or because he is
anything other than a fine orator. Clearly, Gallet's failure tells
us something about the mentality and delusions of Picrochole, a
point to which we shall return. But its significance seems to be
bound up also with the educational ideals portrayed earlier in
Gargantua. In chapter 15, the attainments of the new learning are

ideally embodied in Eudemon. His master, Don Philippe des Marays, promises that Eudemon will show 'meilleur jugement, meilleures parolles, meilleur propos' than Gargantua, a product of the traditional education.[23] In the event, Eudemon does offer to Gargantua a most orderly address, praising him point by point, and the whole address was, we learn,

> proferé avecques gestes tant propres, pronunciation tant
> distincte, voix tant eloquente et languaige tant aorné et
> bien latin, que mieulx resembloit un Gracchus, un Ciceron
> ou un Emilius du temps passé qu'un jouvenceau de ce
> siecle. (**Gargantua** 15)[24]

Certainly, the new education aspires to instil a high level of rhetorical prowess; possibly too, by associating rhetorical prowess with the names of politically great men of Antiquity, the text suggests that this is not merely a polite accomplishment, but can be an effective tool. Nevertheless, arrestingly, within seventeen chapters, we are presented with a comprehensive failure of rhetorical skill to sway Picrochole. No doubt this feature of the text may be interpreted in several ways. For myself, I should say that the tension between neighbouring episodes implies a dual attitude: on the one hand, very keen admiration for the aesthetic quality of fine rhetoric and for at least one concomitant intellectual quality, that of orderliness; on the other hand, a sharp awareness that, in practice, these qualities **may** have limited effectiveness. Clearly, I am suggesting that the text is informed by a belief that rhetorical quality and practical efficacity may meaningfully be dissociated, that good rhetoric should not be judged merely by results. This suggestion is supported, I think, by the way in which, in the **Tiers Livre**, Pantagruel reacts to Panurge's praise of debtors. He is not convinced - that is, the rhetoric has been ineffectual: 'preschez et patrocinez d'icy à la Pentecoste, en fin vous serez esbahy comment rien ne me aurez persuadé' (**Tiers Livre** 5).[25] Nevertheless, he appreciates the speaker's rhetorical skill: 'me semblez bon topicqueur . . . Vous me usez icy de belles graphides et diatyposes, et me plaisent trèsbien' (**Tiers Livre** 5).[26]
In the light of this suggestion, we may look at two other episodes. First, a brief glance back at Janotus. The text makes it clear that his speech is futile, not because it is poor rhetoric, but because it is out of time. It may now be apparent why the distinction is important: on the one hand, for satirical purposes, Janotus is shown as an inept orator; but, because that ineptitude is dissociated from the futility of the speech, the ineptitude does

not detract from the major point still to come, namely that the practical effectiveness of rhetoric **may** be quite independent of its intellectual and aesthetic qualities or deficiencies.

The point probably underlies a further episode, that of the woodcutter Couillatris. who loses his axe and beseeches Jupiter for its return:

> En cestuy estrif commenɔa crier. prier, implorer, invocquer Juppiter, par oraisons moult disertes (comme vous sçavez que Necessité feut inventrice d'Eloquence).
>
> (**Quart Livre**, Prologue)[27]

Presumably, the so-called 'eloquence' of Couillatris is thus described by antiphrasis. His appeal consists essentially of crying 'ma coignée' repeatedly. One is inclined therefore to sympathize with Jupiter, who terms Couillatris, 'ce criart là bas' (**Quart Livre**, Prologue),[28] and asks 'Quel diable . . est là bas qui hurle si horrifiquement?' (**Quart Livre**, Prologue).[29] But the lamentations of Couillatris, cacophonous as they are, are also effective. However irksome he finds the matter, Jupiter accedes to the woodcutter's pleas: 'si fault il luy rendre. Cela est escript es destins, entendez vous?'[30] This episode, by showing a plea succeed despite the execrable rhetorical performance of the pleader, tends then to confirm further the point that in matters of rhetoric intellectual and aesthetic quality, on the one hand, and practical efficacity, on the other, **can** exist separately. (Obviously, I do not go so far as to interpret the text to mean that aesthetic quality and effectiveness are incompatible in rhetoric!)

The question of rhetoric arises also in connexion with the second group of episodes, the forensic group. However, the central question here is probably the ability or inability of the human mind to cope with problems of legality and justice. A chapter which seems to sum up the authorial attitude with particular clarity and emphasis is **Tiers Livre**, chapter 44, 'Comment Pantagruel raconte une estrange histoire des perplexitez du jugement humain'. It contains the tale of the woman of Smyrna, and also some apparently authoritative comment on the case of the judge Bridoye. First the woman of Smyrna, the 'estrange histoire' of the chapter title. Her son by a first marriage was murdered, for reasons of greed, by her second husband and the son of her second marriage. The woman exacted retribution herself, by having the murderers themselves murdered. The facts of the case were clear, the legal position problematical: should the woman be treated as a murderess or not? Neither the Roman proconsul nor the famous court of the Areopagus felt able to decide the matter. From this, Pantagruel draws the conclusion that it would have been appropriate to abdicate any attempt to resolve the question by reason, and instead settle it by lottery:

> Qui eust decidé le cas au sort des dez, il n'eust erré, advint ce que pourroit. Si contre la femme. elle meritoit punition. veu qu'elle avoit faict la vengeance de soy, laquelle appartenoit à Justice. Si pour la femme. elle sembloit avoir eu cause de douleur atroce.
>
> (**Tiers Livre** 44)[31]

Two points call for comment. First, the idea of using chance to resolve judicial questions was not novel: it rested on the belief that, where the resources of human reason proved inadequate, God might be called upon to judge, and his judgment manifested by the outcome of a lottery.[32]

The second point, however, is the alleged insolubility of the problem. The case raises two questions quite normal in a criminal matter: first, was the woman guilty of a crime; secondly if she was guilty, what punishment did she deserve? The answer to the first question is 'yes'. The woman had no authority, therefore the killing was unlawful: 'elle meritoit punition, veu qu'elle avoit faict la vengeance de soy, laquelle appartenoit à Justice'. The second question, the punishment, is obviously less simple, because of the extenuating circumstances: the woman had indeed had 'cause de douleur atroce'. But to treat the question as unanswerable would surely be an exaggeration. Traditionally, it has been a normal part of the duties of a criminal court to adjust penalties in the light of circumstances. Indeed, Pantagruel himself does something analogous in advising the Parlement de Myrelingues to deal mercifully with the errant judge Bridoye, because of such considerations as his age (**Tiers Livre** 43).[33] It seems, then, that Pantagruel exaggerates somewhat the difficulty of judging in the case of the woman of Smyrna.

As for the case of the judge Bridoye itself, we see in the preceding chapters (39-43) that, as a matter of course, he has decided cases by throwing dice. One of his verdicts is overturned on appeal by the Parlement de Myrelingues, and on this occasion Bridoye is required to explain his manner of proceeding. He replies that he is simply using the **alea judiciorum (Tiers Livre** 39).[34] Obviously, the expression does not, in normal legal parlance, refer literally to dice, but to the element of chance which may enter into the deciding of cases.[35] Bridoye, however, believes fully that, in literally using dice, he is following the best legal practice. His dice, he assures his judges, are such as those 'des quelz ... vous aultres, messieurs, ordinairement usez en ceste vostre Court souveraine, aussi font tous aultres juges, en decision des procès' (**Tiers Livre** 39).[36] The obvious satirical point is that the decisions of the courts are totally haphazard.

In chapter 44. the point is taken up by Epistemon. who applies it in an aside to the Parlement de Myrelingues itself: 'pirement ne seroit un procès decidé par .ject des dez. advint ce que pourroit, qu'il est passant par leurs mains pleines de sang et de perverse affection'.[37] Thus, the moral weakness of the judiciary is cited, alongside human intellectual weakness, to explain the haphazardness of judicial decisions. However, like Pantagruel, Epistemon refers mainly to intellectual weakness. In commenting on Bridoye, he attributes, at least in part, Bridoye's use of dice to the latter's doubts about his own ability to reduce the 'antinomies et contrarietez des loix, des edictz, des coustumes et ordonnances'.[38] Thus, the stress finally falls on the inability of the human mind to unravel the complexities of legal problems. And this is very much Epistemon's, rather than Bridoye's interpretation of the matter: nowhere does Bridoye refer to distrust of his own intellectual powers; rather, he appears convinced that he is simply conforming scrupulously to the best legal practice.

In both cases, the interpretations can, more or less, be justified: the case of the woman of Smyrna **is** difficult, if not as insoluble as Pantagruel suggests; Bridoye does appear naïve, and **could** with justification have mistrusted his own powers, even if he does not actually say that he does. The interpretations are exaggerated but not perverse. I take it, therefore, that they imply, albeit rather crudely, a keen sense of the inadequacy of the mind to resolve problems of legal judgment.

The sense of inadequacy is dramatized rather more elegantly in the Prologue to the **Quart Livre** where we see the deliberations of Jupiter and the council of the gods. Although not strictly forensic, the scene is analogous, because it involves deciding between contending parties. Two such decisions are highlighted as being particularly difficult. One is the case of the charmed fox and the charmed dog: the fox was fated never to be caught, the dog was fated to catch whatever prey came its way. The two beasts met. According to their respective fates, the fox must inevitably escape and, also inevitably, the dog must catch the fox. Jupiter and his council felt unable to go against fate, but could see no way of resolving the contradiction. Eventually, on the advice of Priapus, the difficulty was evaded by turning the two beasts to stone and thus, in a sense, preventing the problem from arising or at least from going to a **dénouement**.[39] The other problem is a controversy between Ramus and Galland, between whom Jupiter cannot decide, both being learned men and 'bons compaignons'.[40] Again, Priapus proposes the solution of turning both parties to stone. It seems that, in each of the two cases, recourse to petrification as a substitute for decision monumentalizes - if I dare say so - the debility of judgment. (And since the gods of the Prologue are a very human gathering, it is probably safe to say 'human judgment'.)

Obviously, it might be objected that not all forensic or similar episodes tend in this direction. For example, might not the case of Baisecul and Humevesne in **Pantagruel** suggest that, on the contrary, in the right circumstances, good rational judgment is perfectly possible? Having had all the paperwork burnt, and heard oral submissions from the two litigants, Pantagruel gives a verdict which leaves both sides content, an outcome which the text calls, 'quasi chose increable' (**Pantagruel** 13).[41] However, his contention, before hearing the litigants, that lawyers' arguments alone have obscured the matter,[42] is entirely belied by the oral pleas which take up chapters 11 and 12: as put in their own words, the litigants' pleas are impenetrable accumulations of nonsense. Indeed, the text underlines the difficulty of the matter: for all his gigantic intellect, Pantagruel gives judgment only after pondering long and pondering hard - witness his gruntings, 'car il gehaignoyt comme un asne qu'on sangle trop fort' (**Pantagruel** 13).[43] And the verdict, when it does come is worthy both of the pleas and of the asinine gruntings: it, too, is nonsense. No doubt the episode is a satire on legal obfuscation. However, it does not convey at all clearly the impression that, in the absence of lawyers' cavilling and paperwork, human reason might be relied upon to master legal issues.

One other episode with forensic characteristics which might seem to highlight human powers of judgment is the arbitration by the **fou** Seigny Joan between a street **rôtisseur** and a porter (**Tiers Livre** 37). The **rôtisseur** claims payment from the porter, because the latter has held his bread in the smoke from the roast to flavour the bread. Seigny Joan resolves the issue by borrowing a coin from the porter, striking it against the **rôtisseur's** stall so that the coin rings, and then pronouncing the porter to have paid for the smoke of the roast with the sound of his money. The text introduces this episode as an example of the capacity of **fous** for sound judgment. As Pantagruel says, 'Par l'advis, conseil et praediction des folz, vous sçavez quants princes, rois et republicques ont esté conservez . . . quantes perplexitez dissolues' (**Tiers Livre** 37).[44] Moreover, the text tells us that various legal authorities have thought this arbitration 'equitable, voire admirable' and doubted whether the matter could have been better despatched by the Parlement de Paris, or the Rota in Rome, or even the Areopagus (**Tiers Livre** 37).[45] But is the verdict really so 'equitable'? It is true that it has an appearance of satisfying symmetry: one by-product (smoke from the roast) is paid for with another by-product (the sound of money). But the symmetry exists only in appearance. The porter has gained a real, if very slight, benefit from the flavour of the smoke. But the **rôtisseur** gained no benefit from the sound of money; on the contrary, we may presume that he suffered disappointment, since he watched Seigny Joan handling the money 'en ferme attente', that is, no doubt, in expectation that the coin would be handed over to him. What the episode shows in the **fou** is surely not sound legal judgment, but wit, which invents an escape from the problem rather than finds a solution to it. (In this sense, it is comparable to the ingenuity of Priapus.) 'Admirable' it may be - certainly, it is arrestingly inventive - but 'equitable' it is not.

As for the suggestion that the verdict was perhaps better than might have been given by some famous courts, that is, therefore, less praise of Seigny Joan than mockery of the courts. The disrespect for these courts, superior courts, is of course particularly apparent if one considers the incongruous triviality of the matter. This episode, then, probably does not support the idea that men, even **fous**, have much aptitude for legal judgment; and it certainly tends, on the contrary, to belittle some of the most celebrated courts of law.

It is worth emphasizing these misgivings about judicial judgment, partly because there are quite a few vividly dramatized sceptical episodes, as we have seen, but partly also because of a certain view of kingship which sometimes appears in the text. One passage speaks thus of the just king's dealings with conquered subjects:

> Et plus en heur ne peut le conquerant regner, soit roy, soit prince ou philosophe que faisant Justice à Vertus succeder. Sa vertu est apparuë en la victoire et conqueste, sa justice apparoistra en ce que par la volunté et bonne affection du peuple donnera loix, publiera edictz, establira religions, fera droict à un chascun . . .
> (**Tiers Livre** 1)[46]

In this and a few other comparatively inconspicuous passages, it is conveyed that the good king should and can make just laws and administer sound justice.[47] It is reasonable to suppose that this vision of the **roi justicier** is put forward quite seriously as an ideal. And in this connexion, the sceptical episodes with their stress on the feebleness of human judgment, may be seen as putting into realistic perspective that ideal of kingly justice.

There is obviously much else in the forensic episodes. However, the only further points which I mean to consider are some criticisms of litigants and lawyers which will eventually bring us back to the question of rhetoric. In the course of justifying delays arising from legal formalism, Bridoye claims that, if some time is allowed to pass first, the litigant who eventually loses will accept the outcome more readily. The reason emerges in his account of Perrin Dendin the 'apoincteur de procès' (**Tiers Livre** 41). According to Dendin, as reported by Bridoye, his success as a conciliator stemmed simply from his waiting until disputes were 'biens meurs et digerez' (**Tiers Livre** 41).[48] What the expression implies is **not** that, with the passage of time, the parties come to a wiser view of the matter; on the contrary, it implies merely that they run out of money. Dendin explains that he delayed his interventions until:

> Mes plaidoieurs . . . de soy mesmes declinoient au dernier but de playdoirie, car leurs bourses estoient vuides; de soy cessoient poursuyvre et solliciter. (**Tiers Livre** 41)[49]

Dendin's only contribution is that, by offering to mediate, he helps the litigants save face; he helps each side avoid 'ceste pernicieuse honte qu'on eust dict: "Cestuy cy premier s'est rendu; il a premier parlé d'apoinctement"' (**ibid.**). Thus, alongside more routine satire on the rapacity of lawyers, the text castigates the spendthrift folly and pride of litigants.[50]

This symbiosis between lawyers' greed and litigants' folly is made more interesting for our purposes by a passage on diabolical influence in which Epistemon refers to:

> la fraulde du Calumniateur infernal, lequel souvent se transfigure en messagier de lumiere par ses ministres, les pervers advocatz . . . et aultres telz suppotz, tourne le noir en blanc, faict phantasticquement sembler à l'une et l'aultre partie qu'elle a bon droict. (**Tiers Livre** 44)[51]

Obviously, Epistemon is alleging that lawyers will delude prospective clients that they have a good case when plainly they do not, witness the word 'phantasticquement'. And it seems reasonable to assume that the delusion will be produced by the lawyers' rhetorical skill. In the episodes concerning petitions, we saw that rhetorical powers need not have any great bearing on the outcome of the petition. Here we find the further hint that it can all too easily be misapplied. Persuasion to do wrong is not, besides, confined to matters of litigation. One of the more compelling examples is no doubt **Gargantua** ch. 33, where Picrochole's advisers are shown deluding him (and apparently themselves) with enumerations of easy conquests. Thus, from the comparatively narrow context of litigation arises a suggestion that rhetoric has wide possibilities for misuse.[52]

Another important aspect of Epistemon's words is the stress on the role of evil lawyers as agents of the devil in deluding litigants. The idea that litigants are victims of diabolically inspired illusions is interesting, not only as an observation about litigation, but also because it further illuminates the case of Picrochole. We have seen that Gallet, in addressing Picrochole, speculated that the Devil, the 'esperit calumniateur', might with 'phantasmes ludificatoyres' have instilled in him a false belief that he had been wronged (**Gargantua** 31).[53] The verbal resemblances between the utterances of Gallet and of Epistemon ('esperit calumniateur' / 'Calumniateur infernal'; 'phantasmes' / 'phantasticquement') tend to underpin the idea that Picrochole was indeed a victim of satanic delusions. It seems therefore a reasonable speculation to say that the point about litigants' delusions has not to do solely with litigation, but applies to other fields of dispute as well.

What conclusions may we draw? Clearly, concern with and about rhetoric is extensive: it appears both in the petitioning and forensic episodes, and is indeed the main connecting factor between the two types of episode. There is clear awareness that rhetoric may be ineffective, and that it may be misapplied. Such lucidity serves as a salutary counterweight to the emphasis placed on rhetorical accomplishment in the case of the ideally educated Eudemon. Similarly, there is a clear-sighted sense of the feebleness of the mind in the face of problems of legality and justice. And that, in its turn, is a counterweight to a certain idealism in the texts about kings as sources of justice. And I would suggest finally that, by giving considerable prominence to the influence of the 'esperit calumniateur' and to the existence of characters such as Picrochole, the texts suggest compellingly that this kind of lucidity is an eminently sane attitude.

Ian Morrison   University of Newcastle Upon Tyne

NOTES

1. Colleagues who heard this paper delivered will see that it has been amended in the light of the subsequent discussion. I am grateful for the helpful suggestions which were made at the time.

2. Rabelais, **Oeuvres complètes**, edited by Pierre Jourda, Classiques Garnier, 2 vols (Paris, 1962), I, 70. All subsequent references are to this edition.

3. I, 71.

4. I, 71

5. I, 72.

6. I, 73.

7. I, 76.

8. I, 73.

9. I, 70.

10. I, 114.

11. I, 120.

12. I, 121.

13. I, 121.

14. I, 123.

15. I, 116.

16. I, 118-9.

17. I, 119.

18. I, 120.

19. I, 120.

20. I, 120.

21. I, 121.

22. I, 123.

23. I, 63.

24. I, 64.

25. I, 424.

26. I, 424-5.

27. II, 16.

28. II, 21.

29. II, 16.

30. II, 21.

31. I, 586.

32. See, for example, Rabelais, **Tiers Livre**, edited by M.A. Screech. Textes Littéraires Français (Geneva, 1964), p.293, line 37 and note. See also **Tiers Livre** 44 (I, 586-7).

33. I, 583-4. See also the views of Gargantua about fathers who murder the abductors of their daughters (**Tiers Livre** 48, vol 1, pp.600-1).

34. I, 566.

35. See Rabelais, **Oeuvres**, edited by A. Lefranc and others, 6 vols (Paris and Geneva, 1912-1955), V. 287, note 16).

36. I, 566.

37. I, 587.

38. I, 586.

39. II, 18-19.

40. II, 17-18.

41. I, 287.

42. Pantagruel reproaches the lawyers that 'au cas que leur controverse estoit patente et facile à juger. vous l'avez obscurcie par sottes et desraisonnables raisons . . . ' (**Pantagruel** 10 vol. I. p.273).

43. I, 285.

44. I, 558.

45. I, 560.

46. I, 408.

47. For example: **Gargantua** 17 (I, 70); **Gargantua** 45 (I, 168); **Tiers Livre** 48 (I, 601).

48. I, 575.

49. I, 575-6.

50. On lawyers' greed, see for example **Tiers Livre** 42 (I, 577-8).

51. I, 586.

52. See also M.A. Screech, **The Rabelaisian Marriage** (London 1958), pp.119-20. Professor Screech cites Panurge's praise of debtors (**Tiers Livre** 3-4) as 'an example of a bad cause that has found its advocate'.

53. I, 120.

RABELAIS AND FICINO

A.H.T. Levi

In his recent book, **The 'Moi' in the Middle Distance: A Study of the Narrative Voice in Rabelais,** Rouben C. Cholakian, incidentally to his main purpose, demonstrates how parts of the four certainly authentic books split into what is virtually a collection of **nouvelles.** Rabelais uses fictional characters, including Alcofribas, both as actors and narrators, so that the tempest scene for instance is shared between Epistémon and a 'General Narrator' who also recounts the Gaster episode, while Alcofribas narrates that part of the twenty-fourth chapter of **Pantagruel** which relates the route taken by Pantagruel, Panurge, Epistémon, Eusthenes and Carpalim from Honfleur to Utopia. This switch between an authorial narrator, pseudo-authorial narrators, a fictional narrator, and characters who are also narrators is at the root of much of the comedy and a good deal of the serious ambivalence of the narrative's implications.

The route to Utopia is to begin with exactly that taken by the Portuguese to India as given by Grynaeus in the **Novus Orbis** of 1532, and it is possible that some of Rabelais's more intellectually curious readers may have recognised the route, particularly on account of Vasco da Gama's journey, arguably the greatest known feat of seamanship ever attempted. But the part of the route which follows is imaginary, passing through three places derived from two Greek words meaning 'nothing', one place meaning 'laughable', near the Achorite kingdom, and 'finallement arrivèrent au port de Utopie, distant de la ville des Amaurotes par troys lieues et quelque peu dadvantaige'.

How many of Rabelais's readers could possibly have understood all those allusions in a 1532 text written in demotic French? How many readers even of More and Erasmus could make anything of the Greek roots, coinages and derivatives, some of which Rabelais copies or borrows? Da Gama's route in 1497-8 was well-known; the pseudo-accuracy of imaginary distances is of course part of the humour, like the absurd pseudo-accuracy of the figures in the second chapter of the **Tiers Livre,** but Rabelais almost systematically fills his books with hidden erudite allusions primarily to amuse and parody himself, but perhaps also to declare his humanist literary parentage. It was a learned and elegant game, shared with More and Erasmus, but vividly contrasting now with a register which was not only generally demotic, but which was conveyed in the vernacular,

71

and was ostentatiously bawdy in its appeal.

Erasmus encouraged, and provided material for, Listrius's commentary to the **Praise of Folly,** ostensibly to explain the allusions but really, or at any rate also, to soften the irreverence and any apparent theological daring. Muret wrote a commentary to explain the allusions in Ronsard's sonnets for Cassandre, but what were Rabelais's readers to make of the description of Gaster as the 'premier maistre ès ars du monde'? Why the Greek 'Gaster' (or the Greek Amaurotes which we have seen to help place Pantagruel's Utopia geographically)? With so much research behind us, we can be expected to recognise the allusion to Ficino 'Amor est magister artium et gubernator'.[1] But what did the fashionable neoplatonism of the 1540s and 1550s enable Rabelais's readers to recognise here, apart from a rather robust joke, like the use of 'ventripotens' with its obvious liturgical associations? Ficino's **De Amore** was of course reasonably well known in mid-sixteenth-century France, but with his other major works, it poses two delicate but important problems other than merely philosophical, theological or biographical ones. The first concerns his literary register, which clearly changes from work to work, and the second has to do with the degree of understanding he received, at what level and by whom. The real problem confronting us today is not so much the picking up of yet more allusions in Rabelais's text to Ficino or others, but the way in which the neoplatonist world-view, largely, although not of course exclusively, channelled through Ficino, enlarged ecclesiastical orthodoxy by modifying the view of human potential it implied. It was transmitted through Pico, Lefèvre d'Etaples and others to the evangelical humanist movement, and sometimes purified in the process, as by Pico, More and Erasmus, and it was expressed in wholly different terms and with significant changes by Rabelais, who was firmly committed to the doctrine of free will, as understood by Erasmus, which here means the human power of autonomous self-determination to good. With Erasmus, Rabelais explored trust in instinct as, under the best possible circumstances, capable of providing a guide to virtue. The two really important relationships between Ficino on the one hand and Erasmus and Rabelais on the other concern firstly the transmission of a new view of man possessing free will in the fullest sense and secondly, as in the best of all possible circumstances, able to rely on his own instincts as a guide to virtue, a view of man which could not have been expressed in scholastic terms without making its semi-Pelagianism apparent. Both relationships imply complex problems of literary register, as well as problems of ideological transmission.

Hence the importance of the oblique literary registers and the contemporary reception of both authors. Rabelais's readers will have thought him to have parodied the genealogy of Jesus in Matthew's Gospel and assumed the pseudo-continuity with the **Grandes Chroniques.** They may perhaps have recognised the distinction between the 'praedicabilia' and the 'praedicamenta' implicit in the last line of the 'Aux Lecteurs' added to **Gargantua,**

pour ce que rire est le propre de l'homme,

'risibilitas' being the invariable example in the medieval handbooks of a logical 'proprium', which is always but only present when a definition is realised, while not itself not being an integral part of that definition. It is quite likely that Ficino's **De Amore,** as the so-called commentary on Plato's **Symposium** came to be called, was widely recognised literally and metaphorically for the travesty of Plato's original which it clearly is, that in Panurge was recognised a parody of Odysseus, and that the Erasmian and ultimately Lucianic model for Panurge's mock encomium of debt was acknowledged by accomplished humanists, or even that the reference early in the **Tiers Livre** to the 'vinculum mundi' was explicitly referred back to the **De Amore,** but it is difficult to suppose that Rabelais intended any of his readers to pick up all of his allusions, or even whether they would have cared whether Pantagruel's reference to God as 'cette infinie et intellectuale sphaere, le centre de laquelle est en chascun lieu de l'univers, la circunférence poinct (c'est Dieu scelon la doctrine de Hermès Trismegistus)', a common enough idea deriving from the **Poimandres,** was channelled to Rabelais by Nicolas of Cusa, which is where Marguerite de Navarre got it from or, as Lefranc thinks, from Ficino, conceivably via Symphorien Champier's **Ordre de Chevalerie.**[2]

One of the difficulties is that, even after all the admirable work of Professor Kristeller and the abbé Marcel, Ficino is not totally understood.[3] The **De Amore,** like the **Theologia Platonica,** the **De religione christiana** and the lesser works, contains what amounts to a whole amalgam of myths in an effort to widen the bounds of ecclesiastical orthodoxy. As I have attempted to show elsewhere, there is strictly no way of avoiding semi-Pelagianism if one attempts, without heretically breaching the axiom 'Extra Ecclesiam nulla salus' by conceding grace to the pagans, to reconcile the autonomous power in man of self-determination to good with the gratuity of grace,[4] at least against the background of fifteenth and sixteenth century faculty psychology which, among other things, made freedom a quality not of any act but of a faculty. The psychological description of any act, like the act of choice or the act of faith, which were both cognitive and volitive, therefore made that act either semi-Pelagian or a denial of freedom of the will.

The difficulty in distinguishing between mythical and non-mythical statement persists in the mid-sixteenth century. Héroët was invoking, or creating, a mythology when in the 1542 **La parfaicte amye** he establishes a link between physical beauty, love, moral virtue and knowledge, just as Scève was not making a theological statement when at the end of the **Délie** in 1544, he regards human love as a step to virtue. It may have been different in the 1546 preface to the translation of Plato's Io by Richard Le Blanc, who asserts that even the antique poets were inspired by divine grace, a statement which, if taken literally in a theological context, would certainly have been heretical. But both the first chapter of Sebillet's **Art poétique** of 1548, linking the poet with the prophet and the priest, and the exordium of Ronsard's **Hymne de l'automne**, in which the inspired poet-priest is washed nine times by the Muse Euterpe until his hair stands on end, are clearly mythologising the theology of inspiration in an effort to upgrade the status of the poet. Ronsard openly acknowledged the need to conceal truth in myth in his **Art poétique** and in the **Hymne de l'automne**, saying he was taught by Dorat how to do so, and he continually draws on old myths and creates new ones, while Ficino explains that because Zoroaster, Hermes, Orpheus, Aglaophemus, Pythagoras and Plato 'omnes sacra divinorum mysteria, ne prophanis communia fierent, poeticis umbraculis obtegebant', different interpretations of their common theology later occurred.[5]

Of Ficino we know that he was born in 1433, studied medicine, was not ordained priest until 1473 and, while caught on a wave of neoplatonist enthusiasm, none the less refused to abandon Aristotle and Aquinas, whose **Summa contra Gentiles** he was anyway advised to read by the bishop of Florence, wary of the dangers of humanist syncretism in the wake of the Council of Florence and the renewed interest in sacred and profane Greek authors. Ficino had begun looking for proofs of the soul's immortality towards 1458, and most of the translations themselves of Plato, if not the commentaries, were probably finished in 1469, the date of the **Commentarium in Convivium Platonis de Amore** as it was called, published together with them in 1484, two years after the **Theologia Platonica de immortalitate animorum** to which nevertheless the **De Amore** was a sort of preface.[6] Cosimo de Medicis had died in 1464 and Lorenzo was on the whole less generous in his support for the Florentine Academy. It was Cosimo who, having read Aristotle, was searching for some grand synthesis and encouraged Ficino to undertake to translate, to begin with, the first ten dialogues of Plato and the **Corpus**

Hermeticum.[7] The **Theologia platonica** is above all a systematic refutation of Averroës, but there are passages like that on free will[8] which, if taken at their face value are quite clearly semi-Pelagian. The will, in the act of choice, remains undetermined after the last act of the intellect, which necessarily in pre-reformation theology implies that we still have the power to accept or decline grace.[9] Pomponazzi put the dilemma with force in 1520 when he argued that the will in the act of choice had either to be intellectually determined (as it came near to being for Aquinas, and certainly was in such sixteenth-century neo-thomists as Banez and Medina) or itself cognitive, which is the solution embraced by Henry of Ghent and towards which Scotus, protected by the doctrine of the absolute predestination of the elect, certainly leaned.

Ficino follows Aquinas in his more cautious moments in allowing the choice of the intellect to be influenced by the imagination when it is confronted with a merely partial good, and not its own beatitude as such, in which case alone the will is not free. It is this emphasis on the will's freedom to choose the good or not to choose it, except at the moment of death when it cannot not will its own beatitude, according to the 'passions', 'affections' or sensual appetite acting through the imagination, which was to be extracted from Ficino and emphasised by Pico, by whom Erasmus is still directly influenced in his anti-Lutheran polemic in the **De libero arbitrio** of 1524 and in the subsequent controversial writings on which Rabelais drew.

Pico della Mirandola, who was to be translated by More and whose influence on Erasmus lasted from the **Enchiridion** certainly until the end of the controversy with Luther, speaks of human freedom in the oratio **De hominis dignitate** in 1486. This piece, intended as a preface to the nine hundred theses he wished to defend, is written in a mythological register, since neither Moses nor Timaeus is recorded to have used the words he puts jointly into their mouths, and which, if understood literally, is certainly not Christian doctrine,

> Confined within no bounds, you shall fix the limits of
> your own nature according to the free choice in which I
> have placed you. We have made you neither mortal nor
> immortal, so that with freedom and honour you should be
> your own sculptor and maker, to fashion your own form as
> you choose. You can fall away into the lower natures
> which are the animals. You can be reborn by the decision
> of your soul into the higher natures which are divine.

The conjunction of Moses and Timaeus occurs also in Ficino in the context of a series of books heavily Christianising the theology of Plato, and he records the Pythagorean Numenius as saying 'Nihil aliud esse Platonem quam Moysen attica voce loquentem'.[10]

It is essential to notice how the humanist affirmation of free will in the Renaissance by-passed the scholastic impasse by refusing to write in properly theological terms, as they were then understood. It is arguable that the major intellectual, spiritual and personal dilemma in the history of European culture from at any rate the thirteenth century to the late seventeenth was precisely whether or not man was in control of his eternal destiny. To say he was seemed semi-Pelagian at least: to say he was not in scholastic terms resulted in an intolerably arbitrary concept of God. What the humanists did was by-pass the dilemma, at first by a series of theological myths. It was the achievement of the evangelical humanists, and primarily of Erasmus, to anchor the major humanist beliefs in the Gospel message itself, notably the Sermon on the Mount and the Pauline Epistles. What Rabelais did, especially when heresy-hunting started seriously in France, was to take the recourse Erasmus had had to oblique forms like the satire, the colloquy, the commentary and editions a stage further, serving up, if that may be said, the evangelical humanist message, somewhat modified by its commitment in Rabelais to an ethic in which energetic prosecution of life takes primal importance, in a comic, demotic, coarse, funny, but also heterogenous series of non-theological registers.

The culmination of the strong humanist affirmation of free will comes not from Erasmus's rather unsatisfactory **De libero arbitrio** of 1524, but from the Thélème episode in **Gargantua,** where the famous 'Fay ce que voudras' passage is borrowed from Erasmus's second **Hyperaspistes** letter against Luther. It is also confirmed not only by the ethic implicit in the **Tiers Livre** but, strangely, in the general humanist antipathy to astrology. In spite of Ficino's interest in the occult, he did not let it interfere with his belief in free will, and is indeed congratulated by Politian for rejecting astrological determinism,[11] ridiculed by Folly and decisively rejected by Rabelais in the undoubtedly serious letter of Gargantua in the eighth chapter of **Pantagruel,** as of course also in the **Tiers Livre.**

The autonomous human power of self-determination to good – there was no danger of semi-Pelagianism in assuming an autonomous power of self-determination to evil – was the first great bequest of Ficinian humanism to Erasmus and Rabelais. It was no doubt boosted by Origen and by the two **Apologia** for Origen by Jacques Merlin, one for his **editio princeps** of 1512 and the other, unprinted, of 1522,[12] transmitted partly by each of Gaguin, Colet, More, and Erasmus. There was powerful scholastic support from the Scotist and nominalist traditions, although the nominalists, as H.A. Oberman has shown, did not avoid semi-Pelagianism. There was also support from the stoics, notably from Epictetus, whose **Enchiridion** began with the statement so well remembered by Pantagruel in the **Tiers Livre,** 'There are two sorts of things, those which are in our power and those which are not; but our true good is always in our power'. In Rabelais the Epictetan ethic becomes joyous and Christian. We must act with decisiveness, joy, courage and energy, trusting God to direct our affairs, like Bridoye.

It is here instructive to compare Erasmus's **Naufragium** colloquy with the storm episode from the **Quart Livre.** Erasmus and Rabelais share similar characters and the same message, but whereas Erasmus's characters are cardboard, those of Rabelais sharing the same attitudes are hilarious caricatures of recognisable human reactions. Rabelais is funnier, and a great deal more exuberant.

The second debt which Rabelais owes, however indirectly, to Ficino is even more important. Based on the **De Amore,** it is clearest in the **Tiers Livre,** but like so much else in Rabelais is seminally present in the Thélème episode. It is here that Erasmus and Rabelais, after Ficino, erect human instinct, in admittedly the best circumstances of birth and environment imaginable, into a guide to a virtue that had in the end to be, in scholastic terms, supernatural. Thélème is among other things an elaborate parable. By 1546 Rabelais had to be a great deal more circumspect than he had been in **Pantagruel** in 1532, indicating his own opinion by short speeches from Pantagruel, as at the opening of chapter ten of the **Tiers Livre,**

> Aussi (respondit Pantagruel) en vos propositions tant y a de si et de mais, que je n'y sçaurois rien fonder ne rien résoudre. N'estez-vous asceuré de vostre vouloir? Le poinct principal y gist: tout le reste est fortuit et dépendent des fatales dispositions du ciel.

If Ficino could in scholastic terms not have reconciled divine and human freedom without semi-Pelagianism, by allowing fallen human nature the power at least to accept grace, and so divorcing salvation from credal belief, Erasmus all but formally allowed the salvation of ancient pagans not so much in the **Convivium religiosum** with its invocation 'Sancte Socrates' (1522) as in the preface to Cicero's **Tusculanes** in 1523 when he was writing under his own name rather than putting words into the mouth of a character in a

Colloquy.

Rabelais could not have reconciled divine and human freedom either, but since he was determined to assert both, he too used a literary register which evaded the issue which his own scholastic training had left him, like Erasmus, all too clear about. Especially in the third and fourth books he mixes hilarity, farce, wit, parody and satire with occasionally more or less straight-faced piety, as in the consideration on Christian death, in chapters twenty-six to twenty-eight of the **Quart Livre**, for all that those chapters draw on Postel and make learned fun of the 'Pan-' prefix, yet another case where vast erudition is unnecessarily and often farcically displayed. Both Erasmus and Rabelais were of course condemned, as for that matter were Origen, Pico and Vitrier but with very differing degrees of seriousness and by bodies of very different authority. Only Origen, who had tried to synthesise Christianity with Greek neoplatonism in the early third century, was seriously censured for a variety of neoplatonist and Arian-sounding propositions in the sixth. Marcel de Grève has however shown that in his own day Rabelais was first taken as a simple buffoon.[13] Jacques le Gros in 1533 catalogued **Pantagruel** among his stories of adventure and chivalry. Its first condemnation was for obscenity, on which subject Nicolas Bourbon published a poem in the 1533 **Nugae**. The religious satire was not however altogether lost inside the wrappings of bawdy and irreverent demotic humour. Marcourt tries less successfully to exploit Rabelais's success for more overtly religious polemic in the 1533 **Le Livre des marchans**, with a reference to Pantagruel later dropped from the title.

Rabelais's views became much clearer in the less frequently obscene, better constructed, less episodic **Gargantua**, where the humour was more closely integrated into the narrative, and the boldness hastily diminished from 1535 onwards. Still the Thélème episode preserves its perfect multivalency. It can be read somewhat cursorily as a simple anti-monastery with Renaissance trappings, or as an ostentatiously Renaissance utopian society in which everyone does what he or she likes, but harmony is complete, and it is also a forthright attack on Luther, defending free will in terms borrowed verbally from Erasmus. They were also, not untypically, strengthened in the borrowing. However Rabelais's fame as a doctor by some years precedes the first serious doubts about his orthodoxy and the condemnation by the Sorbonne in 1543 in company with Calvin, Erasmus, Marot, Oecolampadius, Zwingli and Melanchthon. Rabelais was swift to distance himself from Calvin, but the **Tiers Livre** was condemned before Easter in the year of its appearance and the partial edition of the **Quart Livre**, with no reference to religion, was censured by the Parlement. Like Erasmus, Rabelais sailed near the wind and used a totally different series of literary registers to embody the main insights of the neoplatonist tradition, chiefly channelled through Ficino, from which he can be shown to have derived.

It must be remembered that early patristic, medieval and even early modern Christian spirituality was predominantly ascetic. Even well into the seventeenth century Bérulle, in this following his successor Condren as General of the Oratory, taught a spirituality of 'néantisme'. Nature and instinct were to be suppressed, abnegated and mortified in the interests of spiritual fulfilment, an attitude which, like so much else, Rabelais's satire had turned inside out. The sixteenth century abounds in saints who inflicted on themselves horrific penances. It is true that, after the Wars of Religion, when France was culturally catching up with the Renaissance in the rest of Europe, we meet such early seventeenth-century spiritualities as that of François de Sales, who allowed dancing, make-up and whose chapter 'De l'honnêteté du lit nuptial' from the 1609 **Introduction à la vie dévote** was expurgated even from most nineteenth-century editions, or that of Jeanne-Françoise de Chantal whose Visitation Order was founded in the second decade of the seventeenth century precisely for those who could not stand the penitential rigours hitherto associated with the monastic life, and whose lenient constitutions shocked Jean-Pierre Camus. But confidence cracked with mid-century Jansenism, as virtually the whole of what we used to refer to as 'classical' literature testifies, and Rancé imposed an almost literally suicidal régime on the unending stream of would-be entrants to La Trappe.

Rabelais makes a satirical ideal of the grosser pleasures of life, particularly eating and drinking, but he never suggests celibacy whether for clerics or others as seriously desirable. He mocks the contrast between profession and performance, but in the **Tiers Livre**, after Panurge's farcical quest, Gargantua charges Pantagruel (chapter 48) with the mission of setting sail to find himself a wife, so preparing us for the travelogue which is the **Quart Livre**. Embryonically, as with so much in Rabelais, his attitude is clear from the Thélème episode. It is true that the inmates are not allowed to marry, but the sexes congregate, mix socially and in total harmony, and when the time comes for someone to leave the abbey, possibly at the request of his parents, 'avecques soy il emmenoit une des dames . . . et estoient ensemble mariéz, et, si bien avoient vescu à Thélème en dévotion et amytié, encore mieulx la continuoient-ilz en mariage; d'autant se entreaymoient-ilz à la fin de leurs jours comme le premier de leurs nopces'. This passage incidentally well illustrates what is meant here by literary register. This cannot be purely anti-monastic satire, in which case sex or even marriage would have been allowed within the monastery, and it has no relevance to the anti-Lutheran polemic on free will, although it does go in the opposite direction by sharing the reformer's abandonment of the celibate ideal. It can alone belong, with the rest of chapter fifty-seven of **Gargantua** to the utopian level of satire, the tentative suggestion that conditions for an ideal society could be created, at any rate from the 'gens libères, bien nez, bien instruitz', who had 'par nature un instinct et aguillon, qui tousjours les poulse à faictz vertueux et retire de vice, lequel ilz nommoient honneur'. It is the 'instinct par nature' which leads to virtue.

The comparison between this passage and that of Erasmus from which it is virtually translated is instructive. Rabelais hides behind a fantasy. Erasmus, in the second Hyperaspistes letter, commenting against Luther on the much-disputed passage from Genesis VIII 'Sensus et cogitatio cordis humani prona sunt ad malum ab adolescentia sua', takes refuge in semantic ambiguity by including words like 'minimum', 'maxima', 'pars' and saves himself ultimately by admitting the possibility of a 'malitia voluntatis',

> Proclivitas ad malum, quae est in plerisque hominibus non adimit in totum libertatem arbitrii. . . . Fateor in quibusdam ingeniis bene natis ac bene educatis minimum esse pronitatis. Maxima proclivitatis pars est non ex natura, sed ex corrupta institutione, ex improbo convictu, ex assuetudine peccandi malitiaque voluntatis.

Erasmus is careful not to deny original sin, but his exegesis, which he preferred to scholastic disputation as a basis for theological debate, allows him, when the plain sense is inconvenient, to whittle away its content. He was running a greater risk than Rabelais because he was plainly indulging in theological debate rather than amusing and witty farce.

The underlying audacity, however, was Ficino's, as becomes clearer as the channels of transmission become more clearly acknowledged, Gaguin, Colet, Pico, More, Vitrier, Champier and Postel among them. Ficino may have exaggerated when he wrote that the Aristotelian tradition had everywhere degenerated into the Alexandrian tradition denying the immortality of the soul, or the Averroist tradition that on death the individual soul is merged back into the world soul, in both cases falsifying Aristotle and destroying the foundations of true religion, but it is clear that he wished to salvage the authentic teaching of Aristotle while accepting with his generation the whole hermetic tradition, thought to derive either directly from an original revelation or from the Mosaic one. Indeed Moses, from whose visit to Egypt was thought to result the transmission of his doctrines to Plato via any or all of Hermes, Pythagoras, Orpheus and Zoroaster, was also often confused with Hermes. But Ficino, believing firmly in personal immortality, sought what was essentially a neoplatonist eclecticism to underpin Christian belief in personal survival, rightly of course claiming the precedent of Augustine. In the process he was of course seriously to upgrade the capacities of human nature and was naturally attracted to Origen. The original manifesto in the 1490 proemium of his commentary on Plotinus is uncompromising,

> Totus enim ferme terrarum orbis a Peripateticis occupatus in duas plurimum sectas divisus est, Alexandrinam et Averoicam. Illi quidem intellectum nostrum esse mortalem existimant, hi vero unicum esse contendunt: Utrique religionem omnem funditus aeque tollunt . . . et utrobique a suo etiam Aristotele defecisse.

The **De Amore** also was a manifesto, if a more tentative and oblique one. Abel Lefranc calls it 'le manifeste par excellence du platonisme de la renaissance'. The probability is that the **De Amore** is a fictionalised account of a real banquet held at Careggi by Lorenzo de Medicis to resurrect an annual event in Plato's honour which had died out 2000 years previously after the days of Porphyry and Plotinus. The date was November 7th 1468, the supposed anniversary of Plato's birth and death at the age of 81, the cube of the magic number and the square of the number of Muses. In Ficino's work the participants elaborated on the subjects of the speeches given by Plato in his original **Symposium**, and the work was finished in 1469. It was originally dedicated to Cavalcanti, although other copies were dedicated elsewhere and in 1482 it was formally dedicated to Lorenzo de Medicis. The work moves to a climax with Benci's discourse commenting in the sixth oratio on that of Socrates in the original symposium. It is here that we are told of the birth and ascent of love and here that the trichotomist psychology of body, soul and spirit, used by St Paul, Timaeus, Origen and Erasmus among others, emphasises the connection between divine and human love. To a double Venus corresponds a double Eros. From chapter fifteen onwards we are shown how love's object can rise from a merely physical body through the spiritual realms to the love of God. Chapter eighteen is headed 'Quomodo anima a corporis pulchritudine ad dei pulchritudinem elevetur'. Chapter fourteen of the seventh oratio considers the four divine 'furores' which stimulate the soul to the love of God, the poetic, mystic, prophetic and of course erotic impulses, while the seventh chapter of the second oratio ends with the full theory of the double Venus. Pausanias in the original **Symposium** was referring to homosexual love, but not Agli, the bishop of Fiesole, who comments on Pausanias's doctrine in the **De Amore**.

The first Venus is 'intelligentia illa, quam in mente angelica posuimus', the second is the 'vis generandi'. The first Eros 'amore ingenito ad intelligendam Dei pulchritudinem rapitur', while the other impels us 'ad eandem pulchritudinem in corporibus procreandam'. The double Venus is in each of us, 'ibi contemplande hic generande pulchritudinis desiderium'. Both loves are legitimate, 'honestus atque probandus'. Agli is talking of heterosexual love, and ends by explaining Pausanias away. What is wrong is to neglect contemplation for generation, to seek generation with women 'preter modum vel contra nature ordinem cum masculis', or simply to prefer the beauty of the body to that of the soul. What is right is to stimulate love by using the body as its object in order to rise to love's more excellent object, the soul, 'Quo qui recte utitur, corporis quidem formam laudat, sed per illam, excellentiorem animi mentisque et dei spetiem cogitat eamque vehementius ammiratur et amat'.

So the love of a man for a woman which naturally involves physical sexual relations can be at the beginning of the movement towards the love of God and of its own sanctification. The audacity of such a view prefacing a work of Augustinian theology in defence of the immortality of the soul, in which the soul's eternal fate had to be all-important, scarcely needs emphasising. It is for instance far more radical in its implications than the rather dull but abstract and intellectually daring attempt of Raymond Sebond, who died in 1436, to carry the Lullian tradition as far as his famous attempt to prove all the truths of Christianity, including the doctrine of Trinity, by reason. It should come as no surprise that so powerful a suggestion as Ficino's, that ordinary human sexual relations have a role to play in initiating spiritual perfection, needed to be shrouded in such obviously mythical, an-historical terms. Yet the myth was a powerful one. It gave rise to the **trattato d'amore** in Italy. Festugière has catalogued at least some of its reverberations in France. Castiglione does not allow Bembo to regard as legitimate the 'full act of Venus' and is reluctant and concessive when Bembo does allow the legitimacy of kissing among the young.[14] Incidentally Agli in Ficino, while insisting that love must be mutual if it is authentic, also demands that it should be kept to the 'naturalis ordo' and the 'leges civiles a prudentibus statute', a doctrine which seems, as in Rabelais, to beg a lot of questions about marriage and the moral teachings of the Church.

The real innovator was Ficino with his complete confidence in the immortality of the soul, his syncretist theology, and his Christian apologetic smuggling in a radically new confidence in the purely human, in nature and instinct, naturally wrapped up in what were certainly recognised to be fable and myth. The touch-stones were free will in the full sense, and a view of instinctive human love as capable of initiating a movement towards spiritual perfection. This powerful doctrine underwent some sort of distillation process in the mind especially of Colet, who ended by replacing references to Ficino in his works by references to St Paul. It was conveyed to the evangelical humanists by a variety of routes, Pico and Gaguin, Lefèvre d'Etaples, taken up by More who, having with Erasmus undergone Colet's spiritual direction, wrote Pico's life and translated his **Regulae,** by the Erasmus of the 1503/4 **Enchiridion,** and was much encouraged by Vitrier. The confidence of Erasmus in nature and instinct as a potential guide to sanctity is clear, and expressed in cautiously but clearly theological terms in the controversy with Luther, whence Rabelais virtually translates it, makes it much more absolute, and cloaks it once again in an extraordinary virtuoso feat of literary ingenuity, mixing myth, fable, wit, satire, serious Christianity and serving it up mostly as crude, often obscene, demotic fiction. Scholastic argument had been by-passed. When once the opposing views were again drawn up in scholastic battle, we had on the one hand the Reformation, and no single reformer who broke with Rome retained a belief in free will, so strongly were they caught up in their anti-Pelagian dilemma, and on the other hand the Jesuits defending free will against the Jansenists who denounced it. A simplistic reading of intellectual history, perhaps: but I think the scaffolding is the right shape within which more detailed historical research will have to erect the building in its final form.

A.H.T. Levi   University of St Andrews

NOTES

1. See **Quart Livre,** ch 57, title and §2 and Ficino, **De Amore,** Oratio 3, ch 3, title and §1, ed. Marcel, Paris, 1956, p.163.

2. See Rabelais **Tiers Livre**, ch 13 and **Cinquième Livre**, ch 47: Abel Lefranc, **Grands Ecrivains de la Renaissance**, Paris, 1914, p.181.

3. The point has been demonstrated for instance by James A. Devereux in **The Journal of the History of Ideas**, xxx, 2, 1969, pp.161-70.

4. See A.H.T. Levi, **Pagan Virtue and the Humanism of the Northern Renaissance**, London, 1974.

5. **Theologia Platonica de immortalitate animorum**, ed. Marcel, vol. 3, Paris, 1970, Book 17, ch. 1, p.148.

6. On the status of Ficino's works and the history of his life and work, see notably Raymond Marcel, **Marsile Ficin, Commentaire sur le Banquet de Platon**, Paris, 1956 (Introduction, edition, commentary and translation into French); **Marsile Ficin (1433-99)**, Paris, 1958; and Marsile Ficin, **Théologie platonicienne de l'immortalité des âmes**, 3 vols., Paris, 1964-70 (Introduction, edition, commentary and translations into French). There is an English translation of the **De Amore** by Sears R. Jayne, University of Missouri Studies XIX, (Columbia Mo., 1944). Ficino worked on his translations of Plato from 1460-1475.

7. See Paul Blum, **Methoden und Motive der Platoninterpretation bei Marsilio Ficino.** I am grateful for a type-written copy of this paper which I have not yet seen published.

8. Book 15, ch. 8, ed. Marcel, vol. 3, pp.47-8 and see also Book 2, ch 12, ed. Marcel, vol. 1, pp.112-8.

9. The whole matter of the relationship between freedom, intellect and will in later scholasticism is extremely complex. The three essential studies in order of publication are Xavier-M. Le Bachelet, **Prédestination et grâce efficace dans la Compagnie de Jésus au temps d'Aquaviva (1610-3)**, Louvain, 1931; Joseph Lebacqz, **Libre arbitre et jugement**, Louvain, 1960; H.A. Oberman, **The Harvest of Medieval Theology: Gabriel Biel and Late Medieval Nominalism**, Cambridge Mass., 1963. See also T.E. Davitt, **The Nature of Law**, St Louis and London, 1953 and, for the earlier scholastics, Dom Odon Lottin, **Psychologie et Morale aux XIIe et XIIIe siècles**, 6 vols., Gembloux/Louvain, 1942ff.

10. **Theologia Platonica,** ed. Marcel, vol. 3, Book 17, ch. 4, p.169. On the Christianising of the Platonic tradition, see especially D.P. Walker, 'The Prisca Theologia', in the **Journal of the Warburg and Courtauld Institutes,** London, 1954, pp.423ff. Important Patristic texts assimilating Plato to Christianity are Eusebius, **De praeparatione evangelica** xi, 10, and Clement of Alexandria, **Stromata,** I, 22, 150. In the Renaissance Lefèvre d'Etaples attempts to Christianise Plato, notably in the 1499 edition of the Pseudo-Denys, as does Ficino. In the eighth book of letters, see especially the famous **Confirmatio Christianorum per Socratica** to Paulos Ferobantis and the **Concordia Moisis et Platonis** to Broccius Marcellus. See also A.H.T. Levi, 'Renaissance and Reformation', in the **Dublin Review** for Autumn 1965, pp.8-9.

11. For Politian, see Kristeller, **Supplementum Ficinianum,** Florence, 1937-45, vol 2, p.279. See also Ficino's letter in the fourth book of letters to Hyppolitus Gazolti, **Disputatio contra iudicium Astrologorum.**

12. On these matters, see D.P. Walker, 'Origène en France', in **Courants religieux et humanisme à la fin du XVe et au début du XVIe siècle,** Paris 1959, pp.101-19 and H.A. Oberman, op. cit.

13. 'L'Interprétation de Rabelais au XVIe siècle', **Etudes Rabelaisiennes** III, Geneva, 1961.

14. Jean Festugière, **La Philosophie de l'amour de Marsile Ficin et son influence sur la littérature française au XVIe siècle,** Paris, 1941. See also John Charles Nelson, **Renaissance Theory of Love. The Context of Giordano Bruno's 'Eroici furori',** New York, 1958, and Nesca A. Robb, **Neoplatonism of the Italian Renaissance,** London, 1935.

IO·MAIORIS

Hadingtonani, Theologi in quatuor Euāgelia
expositiones luculentę : & diſquiſitiones, &
diſputationes contra hęreticos plurimę, prę
miſſo ſerie literarũ indice:& additis ad finḗ
opis quatuor quęſtionibus nō imptinḗtibus.

Prelum
Aſcenſianũ

Vęnundantur,a quo impreſſe ſunt,Iodoco Badio
Sub gratia & priuilegio, & facultatis theologicę
peruiſſu. a tergo huius explicandis.

QUARESMEPRENANT: L'IMAGE LITTERAIRE ET LA CONTESTATION
DE L'ANALOGIE MEDICALE

Marie Madeleine Fontaine

Il y a de la présomption à prendre à nouveau pour objet d'étude une séquence du **Quart Livre** que la critique n'a jamais laissée de côté: les fameux chapitres dans lesquels Xenomanes 'anatomise et descript' Quaresmeprenant; trois longues listes introduites par un dialogue entre Pantagruel, Frère Jean, Panurge et Xenomanes, et conclues par l'apologue de Physis et Antiphysie; quatre chapitres plus dissemblables en nature et mise en page qu'il n'y paraît, mais qu'il nous faut bien rassembler sous le nom même du personnage qui en assure très fortement et artificiellement l'unité: Quaresmeprenant.

On ne trouverait pas un seul chapitre de Rabelais qui ne mette en jeu la multiplicité de ses points de vue, avec un don tout particulier pour leur stratification géologique, ou plutôt une sorte de génie de la passementerie, les différents fils du texte s'entrecroisant, ou se déformant au contact les uns des autres. Pire: sa 'corne d'abondance'[1] contient aussi un bon peloton de fil d'Ariane. Sinon, 'ce ne serait pas de jeu'. Et l'ambition n'est pas tant de dévider le peloton (à tirer sur le fil, bien souvent on l'emmêle davantage) qu'à l'observer au milieu de tous ces objets qu'il accroche à son passage. Ainsi voudrait-on essayer de laisser en place cet objet décoratif, avec toutes ses inventions - en redonnant à l'invention sa confusion renaissante. Mais ce n'est pas tâche aisée quand l'objet est doué d'un dynamisme interne si provocant.

Du moins les titres des chapitres de Rabelais sont d'une bonne volonté absolue et nous indiquent toujours comment peut s'instaurer, de la manière la plus simple, la lecture initiale; et leur logique, pour les chapitres 29, 30, 31 et 32 du **Quart Livre**, enchaîne les propositions de quelques petits syllogismes assez faciles à repérer: Quaresmeprenant (le carême, ses rites catholiques et son folklore) habite l'île de Tapinois (l'île d'hypocrisie). Or il est 'nourrisson des médecins', puisque le rite essentiel du carême, le jeûne, rend malade. Et, à quoi s'amusent alors le plus les médecins? à faire des anatomies, à décrire la structure du corps, avant de diagnostiquer, par les 'contenences', de quoi souffre le malade. On fera donc l'anatomie dans les règles - parties internes, puis parties externes - mais quand on en viendra au diagnostic, on découvrira que le malade l'est de façon congénitale, qu'il est

contre-nature; car la maladie étant, normalement, un état
circonstanciel s'instaurant contre la nature du corps, si un corps
est essentiellement malade, il est lui-même contre-nature. Donc le
Carême est contre-nature. Donc sont aussi contre-nature tous les
êtres susceptibles d'habiter une île d'hypocrisie religieuse. Et
ils ne manquent pas! N'approchons donc ni dans l'espace, ni dans le
temps (voilà en effet six ans que Xenomanes a vu Quaresmeprenant)
l'île de Tapinois.

Ainsi, il est heureux que la critique ait abordé tous ces
points, puisqu'il faut en faire l'addition, et mêler à l'évocation
du carême catholique, les rites populaires qui l'entourent, mais
aussi les comportements de la médecine et son fonctionnement, car
ils se nourrissent les uns des autres. Il ne s'agit pas seulement
en effet de stigmatiser la pratique superstitieuse du jeûne, mais
encore de montrer sa compromission totale avec les excès de Mardi-
Gras et de la mi-carême, de les affronter non seulement comme les
chars représentés par Brueghel ou les feuilles volantes
vénitiennes,[2] mais de façon plus interne, et somme toute plus
hypocrite: on vient en effet de s'apercevoir que l'alimentation de
Quaresmeprenant, et le reste, est loin d'observer le jeûne.[3] Mardi-
Gras et ses Andouilles n'en valent pas mieux pour autant. Mais la
médecine, et en particulier la médecine anatomiste, qu'en faire?

L'"anatomie" de Quaresmeprenant a provoqué, depuis moins de
cent ans, une recherche systématique sur les aspects médicaux du
texte, qui a culminé chez les Docteurs Le Double et Albarel, mais
n'a jamais cessé depuis.[4] Soumise à l'excès à la structure
impérative des listes, aux injonctions de l'auteur, éblouie par les
possibilités mimétiques du langage rabelaisien, cette critique a cru
pouvoir justifier ligne à ligne dans toutes ses parties un système
analogique qui n'existait - mais très fortement - que dans sa
structure globale. Une telle direction de recherche a pu être assez
convaincante pour continuer à être à la base d'études récentes, qui
tentent seulement d'en amoindrir la régularité, au profit de la
fantaisie.[5]

A l'opposé, l'attention portée actuellement à la nature de
l'écriture rabelaisienne, à sa profusion, son ambiguïté, ses
rythmes, ses systèmes associatifs, ses désordres, ses excès, ses
lassitudes, en abolissant cette lecture naïve initiale, n'a pourtant
abouti, curieusement, qu'à dénoncer le vide de ces chapitres
d'anatomie, l'absence qui ruine le passage, le 'n'importe quoi'.[6] Un
vide et un 'n'importe quoi' qu'on ne peut cependant jamais oublier.
On le rapproche en même temps[7] des expériences surréalistes, alors
que le surréalisme n'a jamais voulu faire le vide. En fait, on
néglige, au nom des excès précédemment commis, de revenir aux

références médicales de Rabelais. Il peut cependant sembler
inutile, et même frustrant, d'en faire l'économie, quand leur rappel
fut un des plaisirs légitimes de la critique dans ses premiers
balbutiements. Comment ne pas justifier ce plaisir en lui-même,
malgré ou à cause de ses extravagances: la bonne méthode ne
devrait-elle pas permettre d'intégrer aussi les austères plaisirs
des évidences?

Car Rabelais a bien voulu nous faire prendre cette description
pour une anatomie, mais son titre ne nous dit pas comment ni
pourquoi. Comme on le sait, l'anatomie est la partie de la médecine
qui se développe le plus, avec la chirurgie, depuis la fin du XVe
siècle, et la liste est longue des textes qui ont précédé le **De
humani corporis Fabrica** de Vésale, et de ceux qui vont le suivre.
On peut voir dans le fait que Rabelais recommence pratiquement son
Quart Livre sur ces chapitres, dans la publication de janvier 1552,
une preuve supplémentaire de l'importance du secteur. Ecrire une
anatomie suppose alors qu'on règle plusieurs questions de méthode -
et généralement, on s'en explique - la première consiste à choisir
un ordre de la description qui peut être pratique (celui de la
dissection), ou abstrait (c'est plus proprement celui de l'anatomie,
mais encore est-il variable selon l'idée que l'on se fait à la fois
du fonctionnement du corps, et de la nature de la méthode). La
seconde question à régler est le vocabulaire anatomique des parties
du corps que l'on est susceptible d'utiliser, selon qu'on s'adresse
à des praticiens avertis, et comprenant le latin, le grec, l'arabe,
voire l'hébreu, ou à des chirurgiens qui n'utilisent qu'un latin
'barbare' et les langues vernaculaires. La troisième, qui n'est
vivement sentie que depuis les années 1540, même si les recueils
italiens ont renouvelé plus tôt l'illustration anatomique, consiste
à choisir ou refuser d'illustrer le texte (qui est, à lui seul,
l'anatomie) par des figures, et à décider si ces figures seront plus
ou moins décoratives, démonstratives, synthétiques ou partielles,
schématiques ou 'réalistes', selon les techniques du dessin même que
l'on souhaite employer.

Sur les deux premiers points - l'ordre et le vocabulaire -
Rabelais a fait des choix logiques et parfaitement normaux de son
temps, sans aucun désordre, ce qui ne veut pas dire sans rire.
Mais, pour réfléchir sur ce qui sépare le corps de son illustration,
cet espace entre le mot transparent (nul doute sur la partie du
corps visée, en effet) et la métaphore littéraire qui a, comme on le
verra, perdu toute pertinence, Rabelais a fait de la comparaison -
ce fameux 'comme' que tout le monde voit sans s'y intéresser[8] - la
véritable colonne vertébrale des deux premières listes, avant de la
détraquer en identité parfaite dans le 'c'estoient' de la dernière

liste des 'contenences'. Ce n'est pas un problème d'esthétique littéraire, mais, plus généralement, de méthode: si l'anatomie était l'occasion rêvée pour moquer l'impertinence de toute comparaison, c'est aussi que l'analogie commençait à ne plus jouer dans la médecine le rôle qu'elle devait alors au galénisme. Dans tous ces cas se modifie le statut de l'image. La comparaison qui ne se justifie plus par son caractère fonctionnel - euristique ou didactique - n'est pas seulement ornementale et aléatoire: elle est saisie par le comique dès qu'on l'affronte au souci de dire les choses. Et que peut-on viser de plus direct que le corps?

De façon simple - si l'on prend chaque fil dont son texte est tissu - mais difficile à lire - parce qu'il en combine tous les éléments en synthèse - Rabelais a indiqué ici tous les points sensibles de la recherche anatomique de son temps: l'ordre, le vocabulaire, le relevé des erreurs de Galien, l'usage de la comparaison comme analogie, et le besoin de mettre en images la description du corps. Indiquer, comme il le fait toujours, ne veut pas dire choisir, puisque l'un des fils directeurs de Rabelais est aussi de prendre ses distances avec tout débat dès qu'il devient débat d'école. Aussi ce texte ne nous apparaîtra pas comme une satire de la médecine, mais comme une manière de la vivre de l'intérieur dans ses difficultés, étant bien entendu que le rire matérialise à la fois la suspension du jugement et le besoin de résolution. Reste à la médecine un sens qu'on ne peut oublier: elle doit donner au malade - et au médecin en priorité, comme le rappelle très bien le second Prologue - longue vie et santé. C'est aussi l'objectif initial du **Discours de la méthode** . . .

L'ordre

Rabelais a divisé son anatomie en parties internes, parties externes et 'contenences'. Les parties internes sont présentées rigoureusement dans un ordre descendant, de la cervelle à la vessie, avec une nette insistance, qu'on retrouverait d'ailleurs dans la **Physiologie** de Fernel à ce moment, sur les parties du cerveau.[9] Il groupe ensuite (1.54-60) quelques parties simples, les 'homéomères' ou parties similaires de Galien: muscles, tendons, ligaments, os, moelle, cartilages, adènes (glandes). Enfin, par l'intermédiaire des esprits animaux et vitaux, du sang, de l'urine et du sperme (à l'exclusion des autres esprits, humeurs et autres éléments cheminant, si l'on peut dire, à travers le corps), il revient à la tête par les facultés de l'âme, sur lesquelles il insiste à nouveau. Les autres parties simples qui ont été énoncées ont été distribuées au fur et à mesure de leur localisation plus intense: membranes (1.7) à propos du cerveau, nerfs (1.16) à propos du cou, artères et

veines (1.31 et 34) à propos du coeur et du poumon, et du foie,
mirach et siphac (péritoine, 1.52-53) à propos de l'abdomen. C'est
tout, sauf du désordre. On peut même dire que Rabelais est ici
particulièrement sensible au fonctionnement du corps et à ses
commandes.

L'ordre des parties externes est encore plus simple: à
l'exception de la notation des sept côtes de Quaresmeprenant (1.1-
4), qui joue, comme on le verra, un rôle important, Rabelais va des
pieds à la tête - des orteils au crâne - sans aucun détour, gonflant
encore ici le domaine du visage, et groupant encore quelques parties
simples à la fin: peau, épiderme, cheveux et poils.

Les 'contenences' groupent toutes les extériorisations du
corps, en réservant des zones successives à l'expectoration, au
souffle (y compris la parole), aux signes expressifs du visage et du
corps, aux excréments; puis récapitule un peu tout avant
d'abandonner la liste verticale. Comme dans les contes de fées, où
les sorcières crachent des crapauds et les princesses des diamants,
Quaresmeprenant s'est livré; et Rabelais peut alors, lassé de la
mimésis d'anatomie, de sa discipline et de son rythme, passer
horizontalement aux moeurs et habitudes de ce grand corps, jusqu'à
en philosopher dans une narration qui reprend son cours habituel -
dialogues et récit sous forme d'apologue.

Cet ordre rigoureux ne nous apparaît pas comme tel pour
plusieurs raisons faciles à déceler, et qui ont aussi un rapport
très étroit avec les recueils d'anatomie, dans le jeu même
qu'entretient Rabelais avec eux, en les prenant à la lettre. La
liste verticale, outre qu'elle mime la figure du squelette, les
'comme' assurant très exactement la fonction des vertèbres dans leur
répétition, rend visible le gros problème d'organisation de ces
recueils: comment rendre compte du rapport du tout aux parties?
Tout le premier chapitre du **De Usu Partium** de Galien essaie de
contrôler les risques d'éparpillement. La liste verticale -
Rabelais le sait depuis le catalogue de la Librairie Saint Victor -
n'a pas au départ pour fonction de rassembler, mais de disjoindre
les parties dans leur inventaire. Or Chauliac, que Rabelais connaît
par coeur, présentait sa chirurgie comme un inventaire post mortem:
'inventarium seu collectaneum', ce que Laurent Joubert traduira en
1580 par 'inventaire de civil héritage' . . . et qui n'est pas en
soi parfaitement recommandable. Mais surtout, Rabelais a dû prendre
beaucoup de plaisir aux listes d'index de Charles Estienne dans **La
dissection des parties du corps humain:** douze pages, sur quatre
colonnes, de termes désignant les parties du corps humain; et
encore n'y a-t-il pas inscrit la totalité des noms communs auxquels
le reste de son ouvrage réfère.[10] L'ouvrage d'Estienne, malgré tout

son intérêt linguistique, n'était pas par ailleurs un modèle de
méthode.

Un des autres éléments qui perturbe la perception de l'ordre
est évidemment l'inventaire absurde des objets comparés aux parties
du corps, mais nous aurons à revenir plus tard sur ce point. On est
obligé de rappeler, pour l'instant, les compliments que Dolet a
faits en 1538, à Rabelais, et qui portaient tous sur le caractère
limpide et organisé de la dissection qu'il fit à Lyon:

> . . . Medicus doctissimus planum facit,
> Quam pulchre, et affabre, ordineque
> Fabricata corpus est hominis rerum Parens.
> Sectum frequens circumspicit
> Corona, miratur molem corporis
> Tanto artificio conditi.[11]

Plus de douze ans ont passé, et Rabelais n'a pas dû tout oublier.
La logique de Quaresmeprenant n'est pourtant plus la même. De
Galien à Vésale, Charles Estienne et Léonardt Fuchs, en passant par
Mondino, Chauliac, Berengario da Carpi et Guido Guidi,[12] pour ne
citer que les noms les plus apparents, l'ordre suivi n'est jamais,
quoi qu'on en ait dit, le même, et chaque auteur justifie ses
solutions en tête d'ouvrage: Vésale ne suit pas Galien et Fuchs ne
suit même pas Vésale.[13] Mais l'ordre de la dissection, qui est
celui de Mondino et de Berengario, commence par les parties
internes, tout simplement parce qu'elles sont plus vite sujettes à
la décomposition, et, dans les parties internes, par le ventre, en
finissant par la tête. L'ordre des anatomies proprement dites, si
elles suivent Galien, comme c'est le cas de Chauliac, commence par
les parties simples ou similaires, puis descend le corps de haut en
bas, les réajustements s'opérant toujours selon l'importance
fonctionnelle plus ou moins grande que l'on accorde ensuite à telle
ou telle partie. En tout cas, aucune sclérose visible dans ce
domaine de la médecine.

Rabelais n'observe les règles d'aucun d'entre eux: il commence
bien par les parties internes, comme dans une dissection, mais non
par le ventre. Il est bien sensible aux parties simples, comme dans
les anatomies, mais il préfère les grouper à la fin, ou les
distribuer sur tout le corps, au lieu d'en faire le départ de toute
méthode. Enfin, au lieu de descendre de haut en bas, à chaque fois
que c'est possible, il fait très exactement le contraire pour les
parties externes. Ces inversions sont tellement conséquentes qu'on
ne peut les prendre pour un désordre, ni même pour un ordre inversé,
puisqu'il soumet sa logique à un dynamisme régulier du va-et-vient

(de haut en bas, puis de bas en haut, à la fois à l'intérieur du chapitre 30, et dans l'organisation respective des chapitres 30 et 31). Somme toute, c'est un ordre du vivant tout à fait acceptable, médicalement, et qui a sa logique de façon normale.

Le vocabulaire

Il en est de même du vocabulaire. On a parlé de son désordre parce que Rabelais semblait mêler les mots savants tirés du grec et du latin, aux mots 'populaires', avec une petite mention pour les mots arabes dont on ne sait que faire, et qui ne sont pas rares: Sainéan avait déjà relevé, outre les évidents mirach, siphac et alkatin, la nuque et les rasettes.

Or il y a peu d'anatomistes, depuis le début de la Renaissance, qui ne se plaignent de la confusion du vocabulaire, alors que le **Guidon de Chirurgie** de Chauliac n'y accordait qu'une importance très relative, pensant que, de toute façon, on s'entendait bien sur la partie qu'on désignait:

'Sed de nominibus non est curandum: dum taxat quod res sit eadem per totum', ou - comme le traduit Canappe - 'Mais des noms ne peut chaloir, mais que la chose soit veue digeste par tout'[14]

L'effort est très intense[15] depuis les recherches humanistes de la fin du XVe siècle: Giorgio Valla, qui reprend l'ancienne nomenclature de Julius Pollux, Alessandro Benedetti, Nicolo Massa, Vésale (plus encore dans ses **Tabulae anatomicae sex** que dans la **Fabrica**, où il a déjà fait des choix), Charles Estienne, etc. jusqu'au fils de Laurent Joubert dans ses **Interprétations des termes et figures d'instruments de chirurgie** de 1585, tous s'interrogent sur le vocabulaire qu'ils emploient, et ses origines. Mais dès les années 1540, des médecins comme Fernel ou Vésale sont très dédaigneux de cette diversité et concentrent leur terminologie dans le domaine gréco-latin, au point d'obliger Fuchs, dans son **Epitome** de Vésale, à régler à nouveau ce problème, rapidement et avec méthode. Cependant, en 1546, Charles Estienne a tenté, avec des moyens bien modestes, et en plein milieu de son ouvrage (I.xcvii), d'en donner un répertoire sous forme de liste d'équivalences: 'De la diversité des noms qui ont esté imposez aux parties exterieures'. Ce n'est donc pas un débat rabelaisien, et l'on peut même affirmer que Rabelais reproduit de la façon la plus ordinaire la terminologie anatomique, telle qu'elle se trouve dans les différentes traductions françaises de Chauliac[16] et telle qu'elle devait être employée par ceux que tous appellent 'les chirurgiens modernes', ou 'Barbari'.

De la terminologie savante humaniste, Rabelais garde les mots grecs (crémastère, pylore, diaphragme, mésentère, etc. ont, par exemple, été introduits par Valla), latins (les veines émulgentes ne figurent pas dans Chauliac); mais tous les termes arabes, et la quasi totalité des termes latins figurent dans les traductions de Chauliac. Certains des termes grecs, comme omoplate et colon, y étaient déjà employés dès la traduction de 1478 (le colon, par exemple, pour le **longaon**, ne vient pas de J. Guinther, comme on l'a cru). Inversement, les ouvrages les plus sérieux ont longtemps conservé les quelques mots arabes que nous donne précisément Rabelais.

Quant à la terminologie dite populaire, elle relève de plusieurs secteurs - le langage commun (pied, poignet, main, etc.), et le langage des chirurgiens (focile, vessie, estomac, etc.) - mais les compromissions entre tous ces domaines sont totales dans la pratique, et un étudiant de Sylvius nous assure que celui-ci employait dans ses cours la terminologie populaire la plus expressive pour désigner les 'pudenda'.[17]

Si Rabelais est donc parfaitement normal sur la partie gauche de ses listes, il ne s'en est pas moins amusé à créer, là aussi, quelque confusion, qui n'a jamais été repérée dans ces chapitres, mais qui prouve à quel point il s'intéresse au fonctionnement de l'image dans le langage, et notamment dans la médecine. En grec comme en latin, le vocabulaire des parties du corps s'est formé à partir de métaphores[18] dans la plupart des cas; et il en est souvent de même en français. Charles Estienne nous confirme constamment ces usages et déplacements d'emploi des termes: ainsi le **bec de corbin** (outil, mais aussi instrument de chirurgie, en forme de bec de corbeau) désigne métaphoriquement, dans le langage courant des chirurgiens, la clavicule, ainsi que le mot **fourchette**; le **corselet** désigne le thorax; la **fressure** est employée pour les intestins, le **peigne** pour la plante des pieds, le **gantelet** ou **gand** pour le carpe ou métacarpe, l'**entonnoir** ou **bassin** pour la cavité du cerveau nommée autrement **lacuna**, etc. Or, si l'on n'est pas étonné de trouver dans la partie gauche des listes de Rabelais les mots **entonnoir** (**Quart Livre** 30, 1.8), **fressure** (30, 1.38), etc., il est plus amusant de constater qu'il a utilisé volontairement à contresens, dans la partie droite de la liste qui contient les objets comparés, des mots qui, dans l'usage normal, désignaient d'autres parties du corps. Ainsi:

Le pylore comme une fourche ⌈clavicule⌋ (30, 1.24)
La fressure comme un guantelet ⌈métacarpe⌋ (30, 1.38)
Le conare comme un veze ⌈vessie ⌋ (30, 1.10)

La plevre comme un bec de corbin [clavicule] (30, 1.30)

C'est donc, déjà, contester l'origine métaphorique du vocabulaire médical, en désorganisant le système des références, alors qu'on ne met absolument pas en question, dans la partie gauche, les mots les plus usités, de quelque origine qu'ils soient.

Plus amusantes encore les petites distorsions orthographiques, dont on sait qu'elles sont le propre de Rabelais, pour les mots **fociles-fauciles** (31, 1.41) et **dours** (31, 1.28) qui ont déjà été bien analysés.[19] **Focile** n'est pas transformé en **faucile** pour de simples raisons homonymiques: le bas latin **focile** (pierre à fusil) désignait métaphoriquement, chez les médecins, depuis la traduction d'Avicenne par Gérard de Crémone, radius et cubitus; en faire des faucilles (ce qui, contrairement aux efforts déployés par Le Double, n'a guère de sens) perturbe plus simplement, dans le jeu homophonique, le système métaphorique.

On sait que **dours**, pour **dos**, est un cas plus complexe, et que Rabelais n'a commencé à l'employer que dans l'édition de 1552,[20] à quatre reprises; que c'est une de ses créations, à partir de la graphie savante en **dors** (chargée de montrer l'origine latine **dorsum**) et des prononciations berrichonne et lyonnaise du -o- en -ù-; que Peletier condamne la graphie **dors**, mais que Sylvius (comme par hasard, le médecin) la défend. On peut douter que ce soit la dévotion aux règles de Sylvius qui fasse choisir cette graphie à Rabelais, qui aurait d'ailleurs dû se contenter de **dors.** Comme les quatre emplois interviennent dans un contexte grotesque, on pourrait aussi bien dire le contraire, et que Rabelais suit Peletier, par jeu d'inversion. Ne serait-il pas plus logique, que, tout en se jouant de ces deux positions, Rabelais s'amuse surtout de la valse-hésitation des médecins dans leurs ouvrages, souvent édités à Lyon, précisément: traduisant Chauliac, par exemple, Panis écrit **dos** en 1478, ainsi que Canappe en 1538 et Joubert en 1580; mais Champier et Falcon, en 1520, et Charles Estienne, en 1546, écrivent **dors** ... Il est difficile de croire à un sérieux imperturbable de Rabelais en ces domaines. En ce qui concerne les chapitres de Quaresmeprenant, il est bien certain que les mots les plus usités continuent bien, à ses yeux, et malgré les folies du savoir, à désigner sans faille les parties du corps, mais qu'il met en cause toute dénomination par la métaphore, dès que cette formation du mot redevient trop sensible.

Les erreurs de Galien

Un autre point très sensible chez les anatomistes depuis la parution de la **Fabrica** de Vésale, point sur lequel Rabelais ne tranche évidemment pas, mais dont il ne se prive pas non plus,

concerne les fameuses erreurs anatomiques de Galien, telles qu'elles
furent relevées par Vésale et âprement discutées dans toute
l'Europe. A Paris, c'est manifestement entre 1548 et 1552 que le
débat a été le plus aigre, puisque Sylvius attend 1551 pour publier
son violent **Vaesanus**.[21] On a déjà noté que le **Quart Livre** se
situait dans les alentours du débat, mais on n'a pas remarqué
exactement sur quels détails grotesques, et bien connus alors, il
avait décidé de jouer, sans prendre parti. Jamais Rabelais n'a
aussi continûment cité Galien que dans les pièces liminaires de
cette édition de 1552. L'Epître à Odet de Chastillon est tout
émaillée de références au médecin; le nouveau Prologue le met
longuement en scène, le citant, au besoin l'inventant, l'approuvant
comme un bon compagnon, auteur de joyeux propos lui-même. Plus
qu'une défense, c'est une complicité, dans un commun idéal de la
mesure: cette même mesure qui n'est guère respectée dans la
querelle des médecins . . .

En fait, Rabelais s'amuse, dans Quaresmeprenant, d'une des
'erreurs' de Galien, qui vient de faire couler beaucoup d'encre:
Galien, trompé par le squelette du singe, a vu le sternum en sept
parties; Vésale dissèque un homme, et n'en voit qu'une; Charles
Estienne se demande quoi faire, quoi voir: il fait dessiner le
sternum en trois parties sur une page, en notant 'les trois pièces
du pectoral ou sternon' en marge, et en sept parties sur la page
suivante, en précisant 'l'ordre des sept os du brichet ou pectoral
selon Galien'. Prudemment, il avait précisé dans son Proesme 'Nous
desyrons l'opinion d'un chascun estre libere en ceste matiere et le
jugement des lecteurs n'estre aucunement contrainct: si que
franchement chascun puisse pronuncer ce que bon luy semblera'.
Belle leçon pour ceux qui, au XIXe siècle, croiront pouvoir
justifier les comparaisons de Rabelais sans se demander ce qu'on
voit exactement, et sous quel angle, à une époque donnée . . . Plus
loin, Charles Estienne assure:

> Cest os ne nous apparut jamais estre de plus que de
> trois pieces: combien que Galien y en mecte sept: que
> nous ne voulons touteffoys estre dict pour contrevenir à
> son opinion comme quelques ungs pourroient bien inferer.
> Car nous entendons tresbien que Galien n'a rien dict sans
> cause: et ne sommes ignorans qu'anciennement on avoit
> coustume de dissequer le pectoral par le millieu pour voir
> le mediastin plus à l'aise: et par ainsy les trois os que
> descriprons tantost en faisoient six: et celuy qui reçoit
> la cartilaige estoit compté pour le septième etc.
>
> (p.22, 1.21-44)

Chacun y va de ses causes et de ses 'observations'. Sylvius, trois ans après Charles Estienne,[22] a montré à quatre cents étudiants que le sternum était fait de deux à six morceaux, parfois, mais très rarement, de sept; que Galien n'avait eu aucune raison de disséquer plutôt des singes que des hommes (les singes étant plus rares) et qu'en fait, l'homme contemporain de Galien n'était pas construit comme un contemporain de Sylvius. Guido Guidi, quant à lui, n'hésite pas à voir huit parties chez l'enfant, qui se solidifient en trois à l'âge mûr. Mais en 1611, deux figures tardives représentent le sternum, l'une en sept parties, l'autre en une.[23]

On ne peut pas s'étonner si, déplaçant commodément le débat du sternum sur les côtes, qui n'ont jamais posé de problème véritable (sinon qu'il y en a sept 'vraies' et cinq 'fausses' . . .), Rabelais décide, à l'entrée du chapitre 31, que Quaresmeprenant possède sept côtes, et se moque ainsi du débat. Outre que Charles Estienne et Sylvius n'ont peut-être pas le beau rôle dans l'affaire, Rabelais s'est ainsi donné un autre motif de rire: son Quaresmeprenant est un singe; et il retrouve ainsi la tradition médiévale de l'hypocrite et du moine simiesque, qui s'est renouvelée avec les peintres de la Renaissance, puisque Dürer brode encore dessus, et que surtout, la figure du Singe a été utilisée dans une représentation humoristique du Laocoon et de ses fils - le dessinateur prouvant par l'absurde que l'Antiquité avait pu sculpter des anatomies exactes, malgré les erreurs de Galien.[24] Même si cette figure est postérieure au **Quart Livre**, elle prouve à quel point le singe a pu symboliser le débat vésalien en gardant ses valeurs anciennes. On avait d'ailleurs noté que Quaresmeprenant possédait quelques caractéristiques simiesques (la double tonsure et le poil follet) et que, dans l'apologue de Physis et Antiphysie, qui conclut tout le passage, Rabelais avait sur ce point quelque peu développé le texte de Calcagnini, qui disait seulement: 'placent enim sui simiis catuli'.[25]

Voilà de quoi est faite cette 'estrange et monstrueuse membreure d'home, si home le doibs nommer': d'un singe, aux yeux de la morale et de la méthode.

Or c'est bien encore de méthode qu'il est toujours question dans ces années-là à propos de Galien, lorsqu'on se met à analyser comment, à la suite d'Aristote, il a pu fonder son système sur la comparaison, dit-on.

Au moment où Rabelais rédige les textes qui nous intéressent ici, plus précisément encore pendant le carême de 1551, l'Université et le Parlement de Paris sont agités de querelles bruyantes. La plus célèbre, et dont Rabelais donne un écho grotesque dans son second Prologue, oppose 'les deux Pierre', Ramus et Galland. Or, en mai 1551, Galland répond violemment par son **Pro schola Parisiensi contra novam academiam Petri Rami** au **Pro philosophica Parisiensis Academiae disciplina** adressé par Ramus au Parlement, et publié en mars: parmi les *auctoritates* que Ramus, au dire de Galland, n'épargne pas (Aristote, Quintilien, Euclide) figure Galien.[26] Pourtant, les attaques contre Galien ne sont pas encore visibles dans les textes écrits de Ramus, et il faut attendre 1556, et même 1560, pour qu'une nouvelle rédaction des **Animadversionum Aristotelicarum libri XX** justifie les reproches de Galland en ce qui concerne Galien. On peut aisément supposer, cependant, que l'attaque contre la méthode de Galien a déjà fait l'objet d'un cours de Ramus en 1551 et qu'elle a été largement répercutée par ses étudiants: dans la querelle, Galland et Ramus font état tous deux de témoignages d'étudiants. Le texte de 1560 est très vraisemblablement l'élaboration plus soignée d'un enseignement antérieur, qui nous ramène au moment de la rédaction du **Quart Livre.**[27]

Le Livre IX de ces remarques sur Aristote, inséré en 1560 dans le recueil de 1556, a largement développé la critique de la méthode inductive d'Aristote, non seulement à partir des **Topiques**, mais encore avec des références à l'ensemble de l'oeuvre du philosophe: la contestation de la méthode de Galien intervient précisément (et de l'aveu même de Ramus, p.78) comme une longue 'digression' sur une citation de l'**Ethique à Nicomaque.** Le texte de 1549 (1551) du même Livre IX se présentait de façon toute différente, et plus sommaire, comme un strict commentaire du Livre I des **Topiques**; néanmoins, il critiquait déjà les 'quatre instruments dialectiques' d'Aristote (la mise en place des prémisses, la dissociation des divers sens d'un mot, la découverte des différences, celle des ressemblances): il disait déjà que rien ne justifie de séparer méthodologiquement la différence et la ressemblance (p.205), et qu'Aristote raconte des sornettes (p.208) sur la ressemblance à l'intérieur d'un même genre, car il néglige l'ensemble des réalités, les causes, les faits et tous les autres outils du raisonnement dialectique, se condamnant à la tautologie.

Mais la critique de Galien qui va découler en 1560 de celle-là est beaucoup plus organisée et forme une partie centrale de ce nouveau livre IX (pp.52-78), chargée d'illustrer la logique nouvelle dans les écoles. Il considère que la méthode de Galien est initialement fondée sur l'étude des ressemblances et des différences accessibles aux sens, et qu'ensuite, Galien a formulé d'autres méthodes, qui sont en contradiction entre elles, quoique se donnant toutes comme issues du principe de l'évidence des ressemblances:

Unicam methodum primo fecit, similitudinem et
dissimilitudinem: scholasticum commentum est: deinde
duas, inconstans etiam commentum est, et absurdius
superiore commentum . . . (p.62)

Galien avait pris ce point de départ dans Hippocrate, que Ramus
approuve, et Aristote. Certes, ressemblances et différences, si
elles sont utilisées correctement, sont magnifiques et retiennent
quelque chose de l'analogie des Empiriques, que Galien a lui-même
exposée, mais elles ne nous indiquent aucune méthode ('ordinis
nullam viam ostendunt', p.56); elles ne doivent pas servir à la
'dispositio' et à l'ordre du discours: Galien confond les matériaux
dont on construit la maison (ici, la ressemblance), et la
'compositio' et 'collocatio' des matériaux (ici, l'ordre méthodique)
qui font qu'on obtient une maison. Platon, comme Hippocrate, s'est
souvent attaché à la comparaison, mais il n'en a pas fait l'ordre du
discours.

Le problème, pour Ramus, est que la méthode d'analyse doit
partir des évidences (pour lui, comme pour Aristote, c'est le
général et l'universel) pour arriver progressivement au particulier;
or celle de Galien utilise les similitudes accessibles aux sens
comme évidences, se mettant elle-même en contradiction avec la
méthode aristotélicienne que Galien suit par ailleurs; alors sa
méthode, qui est synthétique puisqu'elle va du particulier au
général, n'est pas bonne: on ne commence pas l'étude de la
géométrie par le volume, mais par la ligne (qui est l'universel pour
Ramus). La méthode des similitudes ne suffit pas à elle seule à
constituer tous les arts: tirer d'elle à la fois l'analyse et la
synthèse est absurde.

Comparationes sunt egregiae, sed quae methodicae
gradationis spatia illa nequaquam ostendunt: quae quid
primum, quid secundum, quid deinceps esse debeat, non
exprimunt. (p.57)

Bien sûr, les songe-creux scolastiques ont rendu Galien encore plus
dissemblable à lui-même, ajoute Ramus, qui aime jouer dans tout ce
commentaire sur les termes de différence et de ressemblance. Mais
ce que Galien a fait de mieux est de s'appuyer sur l'"experientia",
l'"utilitas", l'"usus" et la "finis".

On peut se demander cependant, de façon très simple, si Ramus a
bien compris ce dernier terme de **finis**, tout l'enjeu de la cause
finale pour Galien et tous ceux qui l'ont suivi, Moyen Age compris.
Il n'y a pas de trace, dans tous ces passages, d'une telle réflexion

sur la cause finale comme justification méthodique du système des
similitudes. Ce dont ce texte de Ramus nous assure, en tout cas,
c'est qu'au moment où, dans leur pratique anatomique, les médecins
sont peu à peu amenés, sinon à contester, du moins à soupçonner la
comparaison et l'analogie, des penseurs tout à fait extérieurs à
leur art, et à leur débat galéniste, élaborent progressivement de
leur côté une critique méthodologique de Galien.[28]

Au cours de l'année 1551, les implications politiques de ce
débat culminent, comme on le sait, et tout ce beau monde - ennemis
et amis - trouve dans le Cardinal de Lorraine un arbitre attentif.
C'est l'année où Ramus, protégé du Cardinal, est nommé à la chaire
d'éloquence du Collège Royal, où il retrouve son ennemi, mais aussi
Sylvius, qui succède à Guido Guidi dans la chaire de médecine que
celui-ci garda sans doute jusqu'en 1548; et c'est cette même année
que Sylvius publie pour la première fois une attaque violente contre
son ancien disciple, Vésale, et y défend Galien, parfois contre
toute vraisemblance.[29] Il est impossible, puisqu'il en fait état
dans son Prologue et qu'il est alors parisien, que ces implications
soient inconnues de Rabelais, et notamment les aspects
méthodologiques. Ce furent de durs temps de carême!

> Gens de bien, Dieu vous saulve et guard! Où estez
> vous? Je ne vous peuz veoir. Attendez que je chausse mes
> lunettes!
> Ha, ha! Bien et beau s'en va Quaresme! Je vous voy.
> Et doncques? Vous avez eu bonne vinée, à ce que l'on m'a
> dict . . . (**Quart Livre** Prologue, l.1-7)

L'analogie et la comparaison

Avec son intuition coutumière, Rabelais n'avait sans doute pas
fondé son anatomie grotesque sur la comparaison et l'identité sans
arrière-pensée. On peut être à peu près certain, en tout cas, que
ce n'était pas pour prouver que la morphologie du corps ressemble
réellement aux objets hétéroclites auxquels il nous renvoie dans la
partie droite de ses listes. L'erreur du Dr Le Double, en 1899,
révèle bien les points sensibles: une comparaison des formes
supposerait que la vue du corps n'a pas d'histoire, et que dessiner,
c'est voir; et voir, c'est observer. Mais lorsqu'on **voit** le foie
en 1538 (cf. fig. I), on le dessine avec cinq lobes, et pas de
profil 'comme une bezagüe'. Le génie, fût-il celui de Vinci,
n'atteint pas l'observation en-soi. Quant aux objets qui sont
censés ressembler aux parties du corps, l'archéologie de leurs
formes est à peine commencée, et si jamais Rabelais voyait 'les
crémastères comme raquette', encore faudrait-il que ce fût une

raquette de jeu de paume en 1552, et non une raquette de volant en
1899, ou un battoir à tapis.

On ne trouvera pas la solution en élargissant les domaines de
la comparaison, de la morphologie à la couleur, ou à la nature du
mouvement, ou à la fonction, ou à la finalité, etc., même si tous
ces domaines ont été utilisés par la médecine depuis les Grecs,
précisément parce que Rabelais moque le fait qu'il n'y a aucun moyen
rigoureux de décider qu'on opte pour tel ou tel système de
référence. Ainsi son texte devient bien consciemment une sorte de
test de Rorschach où seule la lecture est provoquée et mimée, et non
la référence d'une partie du corps à un objet du monde. Qu'un
critique piégé par Rabelais estime justifiée la comparaison 'les
fesses comme une herse', il nous étonne et nous fait rire; et
pourtant, nous sommes encore tentés de trouver des ressemblances
dans certaines comparaisons, tant la science des systèmes de
référence est grande chez Rabelais. Et pour cause: tout le métier
de médecin en débat, et la littérature en fait profession. Il
fallait à Rabelais développer rigoureusement et simplement l'ordre
et le vocabulaire des parties du corps pour faire éclater le non-
sens séducteur de ce qui, en médecine, a fonctionné comme une
méthode analogique. Le rire désigne le litige; il ne le résout
pas.

Dans ses emplois maximal (l'analogie) et minimal
(l'illustration), l'image, en littérature comme en médecine, doit
régler le passage du système a priori fondé sur les causes finales
(qu'elles soient aristotéliciennes, galénistes ou autres) au système
de la description dans sa dépendance étroite de l'observation, quand
celle-ci va cesser d'être empirique, pour servir peu à peu une
expérimentation méthodique. Mais vers 1550, l'analogie - celle qui
a permis, chez Galien surtout, de déterminer l'usage des parties du
corps, comme celle qui, dans l'exposé didactique, permet de passer
de l'inconnu au connu - est encore très vivace, même si elle prend
le biais des traductions. Un répertoire des analogies et
comparaisons de Galien, souvent reprises par les médecins du XVIe
siècle, ou des analogies de Chauliac, aboutirait à un texte aussi
grotesque que Quaresmeprenant.[30] Il révélerait des zones de
références absolument identiques à celles de Rabelais: vêtements,
outils de métiers, d'agriculture, de cuisine, de pêche, de chasse,
de guerre, instruments de musique, etc.

Mais Vésale, qui ne remet ni l'analogie, ni la comparaison en
cause, en est sans cesse gêné au point d'en discuter un assez grand
nombre. S'il reprend, comme Fernel et bien d'autres, l'analogie de
l'arbre renversé, et de ses rameaux et racines, que Galien avait
utilisée pour le réseau de la veine cave, le texte de 1555, modifié

sur ce point par rapport à 1543, grâce aux efforts auxquels les
figures l'ont obligé, doute de sa justesse:

> Hujus venae rami, per jecoris corpus exporrecti, portae
> ramis incumbunt, et utriusque venae ramulorum extrema
> osculis inter se connivent, et multis locis congredi
> continuarique jam dissecantibus apparent . . . Neque
> rursus, etsi Galeno et omnibus dissectionum professoribus
> aliter visum sit, venae cavae rami, ex jecore procedentes,
> cavam in eum modum constituunt, quo radices ad arboris
> caudicem pertinere colligique conspicimus, etc.

> (Livre III, p.458)

C'était pourtant encore un point pour lequel l'index de Fernel
parlait de 'pulchra analogia'.

Même lorsqu'il reprend une simple comparaison fonctionnelle,
comme celle des sutures du crâne, comparées aux gonds d'une porte,
il est soucieux d'ajouter, en 1555, un second modèle de gonds, plus
conforme au système des sutures (1543, f.14 et 1555 p.17). Mais
plus souvent, il refuse d'illustrer la comparaison de Galien et
cherche, du côté de la géométrie, des solutions nouvelles
intermédiaires entre une véritable comparaison et une description
totalement abstraite, indépendante des références. Ainsi critique-
t-il l'inexactitude des comparaisons habituelles, comme les 'petits
poissons' (pisciculi, 1543, f.92) pour les muscles du pouce, ou même
'petite souris' (musculus) pour tous les muscles. Il préfère parler
de triangles, de quadrangles, de pyramides, de cônes, qui, une fois
figurés, lui servent de nouveaux points de départ à une observation
'réaliste' des parties concernées. En fait, c'est la figure
marginale, utilisée à son tour de façon à la fois euristique et
didactique, qui va progressivement supplanter l'analogie et la
comparaison, sans que la solution ait été complètement formalisée.
On en verrait une autre preuve dans l'**Anatomie** de Guido Guidi, dont
le texte ne contient plus aucune comparaison, mais dont le manuscrit
était illustré, notamment d'un écorché. Le rapport entre texte et
figure est plus complexe chez Charles Estienne - comme l'ont montré
les Professeurs P. Huard et M. Grmek[31] - en raison de ses relations
difficiles avec son illustrateur, le chirurgien Estienne de La
Rivière, et des provenances diverses des figures qu'Estienne a
provoquées ou réutilisées. Il dut lui-même, pour ces raisons,
mettre en garde contre leur aspect trop décoratif.

On comprend bien l'inquiétude de gens comme Sylvius ou d'autres
devant l'invasion du dessin: il ne s'agit pas seulement de craindre
que ces beaux livres détournent les étudiants des dissections

réelles, mais encore que les illustrations elles-mêmes viennent supplanter le corps dans l'imaginaire de chacun, rôle tenu jusque-là par l'analogie.

On comprend mieux aussi que les chapitres de Quaresmeprenant éprouvent le besoin de contester à leur tour l'analogie la plus fondamentale - celle de l'arbre renversé - à la fin d'une contestation de toutes les comparaisons: n'est-ce pas la véritable raison pour laquelle Rabelais termine ses listes par cet apologue? Remettre une analogie sur ses pieds revient à créer des êtres absurdes et monstrueux; et pourtant, Rabelais n'a jamais, peut-être, fait preuve d'autant d'imagination technique cohérente, qu'en montant ces êtres sphériques hérités de Platon sur les roulements à billes que forment leurs pieds en pelotes de jeu de paume, et en soignant l'articulation de leurs épaules . . . Preuve supplémentaire que l'analogie, qui est créatrice, n'est pas réaliste.

La figure: reproduction et imagination

On pourrait classer les figures de Vésale selon quatre types plus ou moins stables, et qui admettent des étapes intermédiaires.

1. Le schéma à caractère linéaire (droites ou courbes) donne la direction générale d'une partie du squelette, les lettres A, B, C, etc., marquant les extrémités.

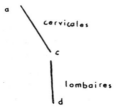

2. Les formes géométriques planes simples (trapèzes, triangles, etc.) schématisent un muscle ou un os, dont les lettres A, B, C, etc. marquent les angles.

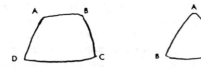

3. Un schéma plus général, sans rendu du volume par des hachures, sans que ce soit pour autant une coupe, rend compte de la totalité d'un organe, ou d'une section relativement importante, par exemple un ventricule du cerveau, dont les lettres A, B, C, désignent les zones dont parle le texte.

4. Enfin, la représentation 'réaliste' en volume, utilise les effets de mise en espace pour une partie ou la totalité d'un secteur dont il se présente alors méthodiquement comme la recomposition. Les procédés sont tous ceux dont dispose le graveur: hachurage, mise en perspective par le passage correct de certains éléments devant d'autres, avec une volonté scrupuleuse de laisser les détails à leur place: c'est la majorité des figures bien connues de la **Fabrica**, amorcées dans les **Tabulae Anatomicae sex** (voir figure I).

Tout le système de Vésale est fait pour une compréhension progressive du dernier état: c'est, par example, essentiel pour analyser les vaisseaux avant de reconstituer tout le système d'une veine ou d'une artère. Le premier état, qu'il appelle toujours 'rudis delineatio' est essentiel à la représentation 'réaliste', mais suppose que tout le travail abstrait est déjà fait. C'est pourtant grâce à cette méthode qu'il arrive à repenser le réseau de la veine cave, et à comprendre qu'elle ne sort pas du foie, parce qu'il a d'abord montré les dépendances successives du circuit.
Cette méthode de composition n'a plus rien à voir, finalement, avec le travail de Galien sur les parties similaires dans leur rapport aux autres parties du corps, et le 'tout' obtenu par Vésale n'est plus de même nature que le 'tout' de Galien. La perception globale du corps n'en est que plus forte.
Et c'est bien ce que l'on observe, par l'absurde, chez Rabelais: quoi qu'on en dise, on n'oublie pas que le corps de Quaresmeprenant forme une masse où tout fonctionne en rapports

♣ IECVR SANGVIFICATIONIS

OFFICINA, PERVENAM PORTAM, QVAE GRAECIS

πυλαιαια, Arabibus verò ουοττα veridhefcoet appellatur, ex ventriculo & inteſtinis chylum trans
ſumit, ac in lienem melancholicum ſuccum expurgat.

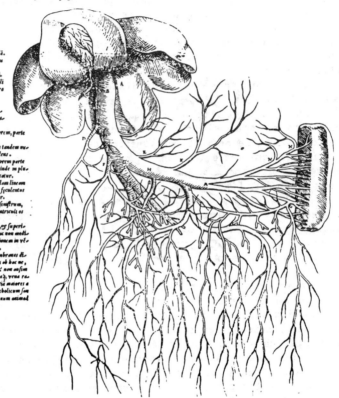

A Cavum, ſeu ſinum iecoris.
B Vena porta, iecoris manus.
C Ramuli in flava bilis veſiculã.
D Al pancreas & cephyſim, ſeu duodenum inteſtinum.
E Ad dextrum gibbi ventriculi.
F Ad dextrum fundi ventriculi & ſuperiorem omenti membra uam.
G Portę bifurcatio maxima.
H Per omenti inferiorem membranam & pancreas delata, variè diffunditur.
I In omenti membranam inferiorem, parte dextra.
K Per ventriculi cavum, ſinus et tandem numeroſis propaginibus amplectens.
L In membranam omenti inferiorem parte media, quę priuram in duas, deinde in plurimas exiguas venulas divaricatur.
M Multifariam diviſa, per reflexam lineam lienis ſinu implantatur : hac fæculentus ſanguis in lienem tranſmittitur.
N Vtraque ad ventriculi gibbi ſiniſtrum, & ſecunda ſatis obſcurè ad ventriculi os procedit.
O In ſiniſtrum fundi ventriculi, & ſuperiorem omenti membranam : hac non mediocrem excrementi lienis portionem in vēnriculum excerni putuoerint.
P N. meroſe inter meſerij membranas diſtribuit in inteſtina excurrit : ob hac ne, an 'à cauo, b, morrbides ſunt non auſim certo affirmare. Nam ex vtraꝗ, vena rami in ipſo portę ptinent, & etiã maiores a porta : nec per portam melancholicum ſanguinem expurgeri forſi dicunm animal vertentis, apperebit. ♣

GALENVS VENAE PORTAE RAMOS PRAECIPVOS SEPTEM ENVMERAT

L. Vésale, **Tabulae anatomicae sex** (1538), pl.I. (Glasgow University Library).

continus. Les deux formules de l'émiettement et du rassemblement qui sont en jeu concourent au même but: la perception globale du corps.

Le dessin imaginaire du corps permettrait de mieux comprendre la dénonciation de la comparaison et de l'analogie au profit d'une perception globale du corps, telle qu'elle se livre dans les images littéraires de Rabelais. Ce n'est pas tant Arcimboldo, que l'on cite toujours ici, qui peut le mieux l'illustrer: sa solution ne porte que sur le visage, et assume encore les complexités d'une symbolique (le printemps, l'hiver, etc.). Mieux que lui, parce qu'il ne vise que des représentations uniformes et dépourvues d'implications philosophiques, ou morales, ou symboliques, Braccelli, dans son recueil de **Bizzarie**,[32] constitue des corps à partir de tiroirs, de spirales, de foudres et nuages, de raquettes, de brassards et ballons, mais sans jamais déborder d'un ou deux éléments de composition (cf. figure II: l'homme-brassard et ballon). Inversement, il peut unifier deux ou trois corps combinés en un seul, qui rassemble dans sa masse les gestes de ses différents éléments, et élimine ce qui est superflu à la perception globale de leur union (cf. figure III).

De telles solutions, qui visent un corps entier dans ses gestes, dans ses volumes mobiles et ses activités propres, ne sont possibles qu'après Rabelais et Vésale, et à la suite de tout le travail des anatomistes, qui permettent, eux aussi, par l'illustration, de ne plus renvoyer qu'au corps - ou du moins de le tenter.

Parmi les différents fils directeurs du texte de Rabelais, le besoin de montrer le disfonctionnement d'un corps par le disfonctionnement de la science chargée de le soigner nous semble tout aussi évident que la distance qu'il prenait - dès le Prologue du **Gargantua** - avec tout système analogique. En abusant de l'image, il la rend inapte à toute description, qu'elle soit médicale ou littéraire, mais il n'en détruit pas pour autant - bien au contraire! - les possibilités de représentation. Ce travail, aussi logique et méthodique que celui qui est tenté par ses contemporains, ne soumettait pas le texte au hasard: il se contentait d'en rire.

Marie Madeleine Fontaine   Université de Paris - Sorbonne

II. Braccelli, **Bizzarie**, f.26.

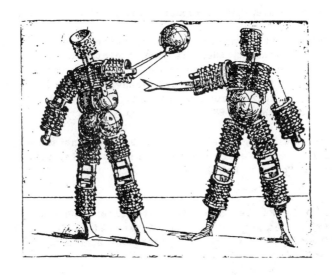

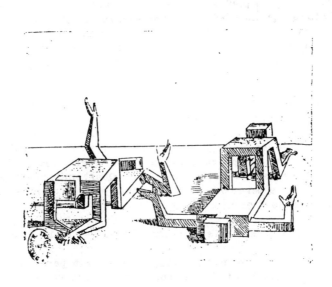

III. Braccelli, **Bizarrie**, f.16.

NOTES

1. Terence Cave, **The Cornucopian Text**, Oxford, 1979, pp.183-222.

2. Telle cette feuille gravée vénitienne, montrant le char de Quaresmeprenant, surmonté d'un squelette de la Mort, et entouré des attributs du jeûne et de la médecine, analysée par Carol Clark. Sur **Le Combat de Carnaval et Carême**, de Brueghel (1559), voir Claude Gaignebet, 'Le combat de Carnaval et Carême', **Annales ESC**, 1972, 2, pp.313-45.

3. V.L. Saulnier, **Rabelais. II: Rabelais dans son enquête: Etude sur le Quart et le Cinquième Livre**, Paris, SEDES, 1982, p.89; et M. Screech, **Rabelais**, Duckworth, 1979, pp.367-71.

4. Dr A. Le Double, **Rabelais anatomiste et physiologiste**, Tours, 1899; les articles des Drs Albarel et Le Double dans RER, IV, 1906; et **Rabelais**, par vingt-deux écrivains médecins, Paris, 1959.

5. Par exemple R. Antonioli, **Rabelais et la médecine**, Genève, Droz, 1976, pp.288-89; malgré des réserves dans **Un aspect de l'imagination créatrice chez Rabelais. L'emploi des images**, Paris, SEDES, 1982, pp.91-92, François Moreau a repris les mêmes développements dans **Les images dans l'oeuvre de Rabelais, inventaire, commentaire et index**, Paris, SEDES, 1982, pp.279-97.

6. Floyd Gray, **Rabelais et l'écriture**, Paris, Nizet, 1974, pp.181-85 ('mimésis du vide et du monstrueux par une écriture, elle aussi vide et mécanique'); Terence Cave, **op. cit.**, pp.208-09 ('an absence, a negative place . . . an emptiness'); Michel Riffaterre, **La production du texte**, Paris, 1980, p.23 ('il faut lire au hasard des mots . . . Quaresmeprenant symbolise Antiphysie parce que la seule manière de la décrire est de dire n'importe quoi').

7. Jean Paris, **Rabelais au futur**, Paris, Le Seuil, 1970, p.52.

8. Floyd Gray, **op. cit.**, p.182, a cependant parlé de 'l'optique métaphorique' et de la 'comparaison qui hausse à un niveau figuratif' les parties du corps. François Moreau, **Un aspect de l'imagination créatrice chez Rabelais. L'emploi des images**,

analyse longuement le procédé des images, pp.90-91; mais la comparaison est plus souvent acceptée et inventoriée qu'analysée dans sa méthode.

9. **Universa medicina ... Physiologiae libri VII**, Francfort, A. Wechel, 1574. Le livre I, pp.1-95, comporte le 'De partium corporis humani descriptione', le livre V le 'De Animae facultatibus' dont Rabelais semble se souvenir à la fin du chapitre 30.
Pour le **Quart Livre**, nous renvoyons à l'édition de Robert Marichal, Genève, Droz, 1947 et à sa numérotation des lignes.

10. Charles Estienne, **La dissection des parties du corps humain**, Paris, Simon de Colines, 1546, f.a iii r - a viii v.

11. On se souvient que c'est le pendu disséqué lui-même qui parle.

12. Le **De Anatome corporis humani libri VII** de Guido Guidi, Venise, Junti, 1611, t. IV (troisième volume) de son **Ars Medicinalis** dans cette édition très tardive, est un ouvrage très intéressant aussi pour ses illustrations tardives. Voir Mirko D. Grmek, 'La période parisienne dans la vie de Guido Guidi, anatomiste de Florence et professeur au Collège de France', **VIe Biennale delle Marche e dello Studio Fermano**, Fermo, 1965 et 'Contribution à la biographie de Vidius (Guido Guidi) premier lecteur royal de médecine: ses origines et sa vie avant la période parisienne', **Rev. Hist. Sci.**, 1978, xxxi, 4, pp.289-99. Guido Guidi est à Paris au moins de 1542 à 1548.

13. Voici, par exemple l'ordre suivi par
Galien (**De Usu Partium**): tout et parties; bras et poignet; jambes; nutrition; poumons; tête; yeux; face; épine du dos; dos et épaule; génération et hanche; nerfs, veines et artères (communs intruments); disposition générale.
Mondino: cavité abdominale; thorax; tête et membres; organes.
Vésale: os; muscles; veines et artères; nerfs; génération; coeur; oeil; cerveau.
Fuchs: os; muscles; nutrition; génération; coeur; cerveau.
Guidi: os; nerfs, veines, artères; muscles; abdomen et génération; parties vitales (cou, thorax, poumon, coeur); tête et vivisection.
Chauliac: parties communes; nerfs, ligaments, chair; os de

la tête; dos et oesophage; épaules et bras; sternum; reins et intestins; génération; jambes.

Charles Estienne, quant à lui, revient souvent en arrière. Johannes Guinther conseillait à ses étudiants l'ordre de la dissection comme le plus conforme aux médecins antérieurs à Galien.

14. Traduction de Canappe, Lyon, Guillaume de Guelques, 1538, f.45r. (Le Guidon en Françoys).

15. Voir notamment Ch. Singer et C. Rabin, A prelude to modern science, being a discussion of the history, sources and circumstances of the 'Tabulae anatomicae sex' of Vesalius, Wellcome Hist. Med. Mus., Cambridge, 1946; et O'Malley, Andreas Vesalius of Brussels, Berkeley, Los Angeles, Univ. of California Press, 1964. Voir aussi le dictionnaire d'Henri Estienne; et J. Hyrtl, Das Arabische und Hebräische in der Anatomie, Wien, 1879, et Onomatologia anatomica . . . , Wien, 1880.

16. Par Nicolas Panis, Lyon, B. Buyer, 1478; Symphorien Champier et J. Falcon, Lyon, Constantin Fradin, 1520; J. Canappe, Lyon, Guillaume de Guelques, 1538; Laurent Joubert, Lyon, Etienne Michel, 1580.

17. Dans O'Malley, op. cit. Voir Renatus Henerus et Du Fail.

18. Voir J. Irigoin, 'La formation du vocabulaire de l'anatomie en grec: du mycénien aux principaux traités de la collection hippocratique', Hippocratica, Paris, 1980, pp.247-56; et Diego Lanza, 'Quelques remarques sur le travail linguistique du médecin', Formes de pensée dans la Collection hippocratique, Actes du IVe Colloque international hippocratique (Lausanne, 21-2 sept. 1981), ed. F. Lasserre et Ph. Mudry, Genève, Droz, 1983, pp.181-85.

19. Pour 'focile', voir F. Moreau, op. cit., Inventaire . . . , p.291. Pour 'dours', voir Mireille Huchon, Rabelais grammairien, Etudes Rabelaisiennes, t. XVI, Genève, Droz, 1981, pp.230-33.

20. M. Huchon, op. cit., p.231. Sur les prononciations, voir aussi R. Lathuillère, 'Un grammairien lyonnais du XVIe siècle, Claude Mermet et le problème de l'orthographe', L'Humanisme Lyonnais

au **XVIe siècle**, Presses Universitaires de Grenoble, 1974, pp.261-73 (-o- et -ù-, p.271).

21. **Vaesani cujusdam Calumniarum in Hippocratis Galenique rem anatomicam depulsio**, Paris, 1551. Voir O'Malley, **op. cit.**

22. **De ossibus ad tyrones** (de Galien), 1549, p.47.

23. Guido Guidi, **De Anatome**, 1611, pp.47-48.

24. Voir H.W. Janson, **Apes and ape lore in the Middle Ages and Renaissance**, Londres, 1952. **La danse des singes** de Dürer est de 1523. Voir aussi Mario Vegetti, **Tra Edipo e Euclide**, L'Arco 13, Milan, Il Saggiatore, 1983, ch.3 'L'animale ridicolo'.
    On peut ajouter que le singe désigne, dans les cinq sens, le goût, ce qui convient bien au problème du Carême.
    Massa avait déjà été attentif aux différences entre le singe et l'homme dans son **Anathomiae Liber introductorius** de 1536.

25. Voir M. Screech, **op. cit.**, p.368; et pour les additions de Rabelais à Calcagnini, Richard Cooper, 'Les "contes" de Rabelais et l'Italie: une mise au point', **La nouvelle française à la Renaissance**, ed. Lionello Sozzi, Slatkine, 1981, pp.183-207 (pp.196-98).

26. pp.3 et 69.

27. Pour la méthode de Ramus et sa critique de Galien, voir W.J. Ong, **Ramus, Method and the Decay of Dialogue**, Harvard Univ. Press, Cambridge, Mass., 1958, ch. XI, et notamment pp.257-58; et surtout Neal W. Gilbert, **Renaissance Concepts of Method**, Columbia Univ. Press, New York, 1960, pp.137-42.

28. Sur la philosophie de Galien, voir notamment O. Temkin, **Galenism**, Ithaca, London, Cornell Univ. Press, 1970; Paul Moraux, 'Galien comme philosophe: la philosophie de la nature', et Andrew Wear, 'Galen in the Renaissance', in **Galen: problems and prospects**, ed. Vivian Nutton, Wellcome Inst. Hist. Med., 1981, pp.87-116 et 229-62.

29. Voir notes 21 et 22.

30. Voici quelques analogies et comparaisons de la traduction du **De Usu Partium** par Claude Dalechamps, Lyon, Rouillé, 1566: le

corps comme les marionnettes (47), les tendons du poignet comme
les courroies ou rènes d'un joug à boeuf (53), le cheminement
de la nourriture par grands chemins, puis ruelles, sentiers,
passages étroits (211-12), les veines comme approvisionnement
des villes (213), le tri des aliments comme dépôt de la lie du
vin au fond du tonneau (214), la veine du foie comme un aqueduc
ou un char (217), l'estomac comme un égouttoir (220), les
tuniques de l'estomac comme des mains pour attirer (223),
l'épine dorsale comme un rempart, les muscles comme un coussin
(225), les muscles de l'abdomen comme une haie (228), etc.
Et dans la traduction de Chauliac par Canappe, 1538:
les épaules comme une bec de corbin (33 v), la 'boete ou fosse
de l'épaule' comme la poulie double d'un puits (33 v), le coeur
en forme de pomme de pin (33 r), l'estomac en forme de
cucurbite (39 r), la rotule comme une meule de moulin (45 v),
l'astragale comme un noeud d'arbalète (46 r), etc.
Quant à Charles Estienne, il en a fait volontairement
collection. Fernel conserve le sternum en forme de carène de
navire, qui vient de Galien, l'arbre des veines; mais ses
comparaisons et analogies sont déjà rares.

31. Pierre Huard et Mirko D. Grmek, 'L'oeuvre de Charles Estienne
     et l'Ecole anatomique parisienne', Préface à l'édition
     facsimile de La dissection des parties du corps humain, Paris,
     Cercle du livre précieux, 1972.

32. Giovanbattista Braccelli, Bizzarie di varie Figure, 1607; le
     recueil est dessiné dans la deuxième moitié du XVIe siècle et
     offert à Pierre de Médicis.

STULTORUM NUMERUS INFINITUS:
Attitudes to Folly in the Sixteenth Century and in Rabelais

Carol Clark

In chapter 46 of the **Tiers Livre** Pantagruel, interpreting the prophecy of Triboulet, tells Panurge that he is **fol**:

> Et quel fol? Fol enraigé, qui sus vos vieulx jours voulez
> en mariage vous lier et asservir.

In all the preceding consultation episodes Panurge has contradicted Pantagruel's interpretations, and here too he indignantly denies that he will be cuckolded and robbed. But his folly (or madness) he cannot deny:

> Non que je me veuille impudentement exempter du territoire
> de follie, j'en tiens et en suys, je le confesse. Tout le
> monde est fol. En Lorraine Fou est pres Tou, par bonne
> discretion. Tout est fol. Solomon dict que infini est
> des folz le nombre. A infinité rien ne peut decheoir,
> rien ne peut estre adjoinct, comme prouve Aristoteles, et
> fol enragé serois si, fol estant, fol ne me reputois.

The words Panurge quotes here ('Stultorum infinitus est numerus', Ecclesiastes I, 15) must have been one of the best-known Biblical texts of Rabelais's day. It is continually cited in the most diverse contexts - as a text for real sermons preached in church and for outrageous parody sermons delivered at the meetings of fool-societies, as a motto on seals and banners of such societies and a legend on woodcuts and engravings from the smallest and cheapest to the most elaborate and expensive.[1] To quote but one example among many, Sir David Lindsay's **Satire of the Thrie Estaits**, first acted before the Scottish court on Twelfth-Day, 1540, ends with a sermon preached by Folie, which begins thus:

> STULTORUM NUMERUS INFINITUS
> Salomon, the maist sapient king
> In Israell, quhan he did ring,
> Thir words, in effect, did write,
> THE NUMBER OF FUILLIS AR INFINITE.
> I think na schame, sa Christ me saife,

113

STULTORUM NUMERUS INFINITUS

To be ane Fuill, amang the laife,
Howbeit, an hundreth stands heir by
Perventure, als great fuillis as I.

Folly proceeds to distribute 'Folie Hattis' (fools' caps) to the
audience: among the first in line for them is the man who is 'baith
auld and cauld', and who yet 'taks ane lasse to be his peir'
trusting that she will not 'rycht hastelie make him cuckald'.

In this paper I propose to explore some of the different things
this famous text may have meant to the various speakers and writers
who quoted it, and to their audiences; for just as **stultus** or **fol**
carried a wide range of meanings in the sixteenth century,[2] the
notion that all men are to some extent foolish (or mad) could be
used to point to a variety of conclusions.

In the early part of the sixteenth century, the best-known
printed treatment of folly in the European vernaculars was certainly
Sebastian Brant's **Ship of Fools**. First published in German in 1494,
it was quickly translated into Latin, French, English and Dutch, and
soon enjoyed a wide reputation based as much, some critics say, on
its lively woodcuts as on its decidedly stodgy text.[3] Each of its
chapters depicts a different kind of fool, but Brant at one moment
attacks grave vices and at the next mere frivolities like book-
collecting or serenading ladies. For him the number of fools is
indeed infinite, for there are few kinds of human behaviour that he
would not lump together under the all-purpose title of folly. The
Ship of Fools is sometimes described as a satire, but it is doubtful
whether it deserves this title, for there is little humour in it;
it is, rather, an ill-organised list of all the human failings to
which a sober-minded, middle-aged man of conservative moral outlook
could possibly take exception.

Even more moralistic, however, is the series of a hundred and
ten sermons, based on Brant's chapters, which the famous preacher
Johann Geiler von Kaysersberg delivered at Strasbourg in 1498, and
which were translated into Latin and published in 1510 under the
title **Navicula, sive speculum fatuorum**.[4] Almost every one of these
sermons has Ecclesiastes I, 15 as its text, and Geiler extends the
range of meaning of **stultitia** even further than Brant had done.
Indeed, it seems as if for him every kind of behaviour having
anything but salvation as its immediate object is a form of
stultitia. The first sermon is a good example of his methods:
whereas Brant had taken as his first fool the man who collects books
in large numbers but does not read them, Geiler attacks all book
collectors, even those who seek them out 'propter scientiam
acquirendam'. Brant had criticised men who contracted unsuitable

marriages for money: Geiler attacks not only those who wish to marry 'propter delitias: voluptatem: pulchritudinem etc.', but even those who do so 'propter generationem prolis mundane' or 'propter vitationem fornicationis' (ch. 51). A 'worldly' marriage for him is one contracted 'propter generationem prolis: non tamen educande ad cultum dei sed mundi. Ut habent aliquem sui nominis haeredem et posteritatem propagent'. Under the heading of 'building fools' and its subheadings 'edificare multa: edificare magna: edificare sumptuosa: edificare delectabilia', Geiler attacks the designing of luxurious, spacious and even convenient lodgings: 'fons canalibus in coquinam dirigitur: et alia sexcenta talia mollia. Sed numquid et haec stultitia est' (chapter 15). Travel ('lustrare ex sola curiositate', chapter 65), study of the poets (Ovid, Propertius, Tibullus 'turpissimus sodomita' and even Virgil, ch. 26) and of the sciences are condemned as folly (chapter 66, of fools 'presumentium se sapientes esse', is illustrated by a picture of a dissection). How much more so then are greed and a taste for drink and low jokes (see chapter 16, 'Potatorum et gulosorum', with its subheadings of 'inepta letitia', 'loquacitas', 'scurrilitas' and 'immunditia'). Rabelais, one feels, would have got short shrift at the hands of Dr Geiler.

Not all sixteenth-century writers on folly, however, take this uncompromisingly censorious attitude to it. Erasmus's **Praise of Folly**, as is well known, is a declamation - a kind of sermon[5] - delivered by Folly herself. It is thus (designedly) difficult for us to evaluate the points the speaker makes, and to know precisely what attitude the author, hidden behind the speaker, is himself taking. But Folly is allowed some clever scores off the wise (including Erasmus himself and his humanist colleagues), and it does appear as if some of the kinds of folly she lists (childish prattling, lovers' foolishness, old men's illusions - even the follies of hunters, builders or gamblers) are meant to be viewed with more indulgence than the murderous follies of, say, warlike popes.

As well as straightforward translations there were various vernacular imitations of the **Praise of Folly** in the mid-sixteenth century, for example Vianesio Albergati's **La Pazzia**,[6] first published around 1540, and the French translation of it made by Jean du Thier (Ronsard's patron) and published after his death in 1566 under the title **Les louanges de la folie.** The few twentieth-century critics who have mentioned Albergati's work describe it as a partial translation of the **Praise of Folly,** but this is not altogether accurate. Its opening pages do follow Erasmus fairly closely, but the rest diverges quite sharply. The intellectual satire of the

Praise of Folly (the sections on philosophers and theologians for example) is largely omitted, as are of course the angry attacks on the Papal court and on Julius II. The whole final section on ecstatic folly and the folly of the Cross likewise disappears. In their place we find the section on the follies of women greatly expanded (with some lively pages on the **femmes savantes** of the Cinquecento), and more attention paid to contemporary, secular examples of folly: not only Erasmus's builders, hunters and gamblers but litigants, merchants, sailors and the disreputable family of charlatans, alchemists, fortune-tellers, necromancers and believers in witchcraft. The concluding example is that of linguistic pedants, trying to set rules for writing in the **lingua volgare.**

Albergati has some of Erasmus's problems in focussing his satire, and he lacks Erasmus's finesse in solving or side-stepping them. Ostensibly praising folly, he finds himself lampooning particular examples of it; but his general theme is that folly is harmless, and indeed a source of happiness to men. He almost reaches eloquence in the pages he devotes to the happy life of the American Indians before the coming of the 'Spagnoli troppo savii', and to folly as man's last remedy against the tribulations of old age.

We may like to compare Albergati's work with a pictorial treatment of folly like the print **L'Arboro della Pazzia.**[7] This large print shows many small scenes of folly, disposed as if along the branches of a tree. At the foot of the tree, in a cartouche framed by figures of satyrs, is the verse:

Alla dolce ombra de l'altiera pianta
che da lorto al ocaso i rami estende
Ciaschuno che qua giu viver savanta [si vanta?]
o voglia o no per tempo tardi sende [scende?]
Chiunque travaglia burla ride o canta
Desta radice rami o frutti prende
Chi le fronde chi all'ombra star desia
che par a tutti dolce la pazzia.

The fools depicted are drawn from every walk of life: we encounter not only the lovers, litigants, soldiers, sailors, hunters, merchants, gamblers, diviners, astrologers, alchemists and charlatans of Albergati, but princes and judges, mathematicians, orators, philosophers and poets and even fishermen, farmers and shepherds. What do all these characters have in common, one wonders, apart from their common humanity? Perhaps it is the fact that they all put faith in the future, and have to rely on chance or luck. But few human beings are lucky enough to escape such a dependence! There seems to me to be also a strong suggestion in this print that the more powerful characters at least are fools precisely because they consider themselves wise, and able to defy the powers of fate. At the bottom left of the picture we see boys mocking a fool, a kind of village idiot who is baring his backside. The legend reads: 'Degno di riso è certamente un pazzo / Ma per dar fine in somma al mio concetto / Pazzo e tenuto qual piu savio e detto'.

This theme - that the wisest men, or those who think themselves most wise, are really the greatest fools - recurs constantly in vernacular writing about folly, and may take the neat form of asserting that anyone who criticises what he is reading on the grounds of its folly is thereby showing himself a greater fool than the author. The text of **La pazzia** ends:

> Ma per esser [i pazzi] in numer grandissimi, lasciamoli goder del privilegio della vera pazzia, acciochel piu pazzo piu savio si reputi, e di sua pazzia piu si goda.

and the colophon (present in most but not all editions) reads:

> Stampato in India Pastinaca, per Messer Non mi biasimate, al uscire delle Mascare et delle Pazzie Carnevalesche. Con Gratia Et Privilegio di tutti i cervelli heterocliti et con espresso protesto che chiunque di questa Pazzia dirà male, s'intenda d'allhora in poi essere Pazzo da dovero quantunque per tale non fosse conosciuto.

(Compare Rabelais's retort to his readers in **Pantagruel** 34:

> Si vous me dictes: 'Maistre, il sembleroit que ne feussiez grandement saige de nous escrire ces balivernes et plaisantes moquettes', je vous responds que ne l'estes guères plus de vous amuser à les lire).

The Douce collection includes several prints on the theme of folly with legends similarly designed to draw the viewer into the company of fools.[8] One, from the French sixteenth century, shows four fools looking out, apparently from a barred window; one of them is pointing a finger at the viewer, and the legend is 'Nous sommes cinq'.[9] Another later print creates a complicated pattern of

fools and asses; by counting heads and legs, one works out that
there are three fools and three asses in the picture, but the legend
is 'Nous sommes sept'.[10] Even a sober compilation like Guillaume de
la Perrière's **La Morosophie** of 1553 (which has nothing foolish about
it but its title) bears the prefatory verses:

> Comme chacun sait par usage,
> Que n'est si bon vin qui n'ait lye,
> Aussi n'est il homme si sage,
> Qui n'ait contrepois de folie.

How wise men (or, more likely, revellers impersonating wise
men) might figure in celebrations of folly, and in what strange
company they might then appear, is shown by the surviving plans for
the Christmas celebrations at the court of Edward VI in 1552.
George Ferrers, who was to play the Lord of Misrule, wrote to the
Master of the Revels suggesting the form his appearance might take.
He offered to arrive

> . . . under a Canepie as the last yeare, or in a chare
> triumphall, or uppon some straunge beaste that I reserve
> to you / But the serpent with seven heddes called hidra is
> the chief beast of myne armes / and the wholie bushe is
> the devise of my Crest / my worde is **semper ferians** /
> alwaies feasting or keping holie daie.
> Uppon Christmas daie I sende a solempe ambassade to
> the kinges Maiestie by an herralds trumpet an orator
> speaking in a straunge language an Interpreter or a
> truchman with him . . . [also two drummers to be]
> aparelled like turkes . . .

On St Stephen's Day (Boxing Day) he proposed to be attended by
'a divine a philosopher an astronomer a poet a physician a potecarie
/ a Mr of requestes / a sivilian [i.e. a civil lawyer] / a disard /
two Gentlmen ushers besides Iuglers / tumblers / fooles / friers and
such other'. (The bills survive for the costumes of these
attendants; the wise men wore cloth gowns at 2s 8d the gown, while
the fools were dressed more magnificently in 'crimesene taffita
lined with goulde silver and yellow sarcenet with hoods of the
same', at 3s 4d.)[11]
The mention of such festivities leads us to the third kind of
vernacular writing about folly that is important as a background to
Rabelais's book: the writing that openly celebrates folly as a
state not only universal but desirable. 'Writing' is perhaps a

misnomer here, for I am referring to printed texts which preserve
(no doubt in fragmentary form) visual and oral (not to say potatory
and gustatory) events like the meetings of fool-societies. These
societies met at fixed times of the year; their **raison d'être**
appears to have been communal celebration, but their rationale, as
expressed for example in the **cris** which summoned the fools together,
was the familiar one of **stultorum numerus infinitus**, or as a fool-
preacher once put it,

> Puisque la plus grande partie
> Du monde est subjecte a folye,
> Pensons à folye satisfaire . . . [12]

It is suggested that the dramatic form of the **sermon joyeux** is
associated with the institution of fool-societies. Jacobsen in **La
comédie en France au moyen âge** says that such sermons were probably
preached 'dans les assemblées des sociétés badines, dans les
réunions de clercs du Palais, dans les repas et spécialement dans
les repas de noces'.[13] Certainly Ecclesiastes I, 15 is the
favourite text of the burlesque preacher: it opens, for example,
the **Sermon de sainct Jambon et de ma Dame Saincte Andouille.**[14] The
**Sermon joyeux et de grant value à tous les foulx qui sont dessoubz
la nue** includes not only this text but no fewer than thirteen other
Biblical quotations ('Cogitationes hominum vanae sunt; Vae qui
sapientes estis in oculis vestris; Multi sunt vocati pauci vero
electi; Sapientia huius mundi stultitia est' and so forth); all,
however, cited in the context of the most indecent badinage about
lovers and husbands. The speaker in this sermon maintains that

> Les plus sots et enragez foulx
> Qui sont au monde, ce sont jaloux.

It is not these disagreeable fools that he is inviting to the
festivities, but cheerful fools who accept the inevitability of
cuckoldry and drown their sorrows in wine and good fellowship.

On this spectrum of attitudes, from the stern punitiveness of
Brant and Geiler, through the ambiguous ironies of Erasmus and his
imitators, to the fool-preachers' wholehearted embracing of folly,
where does Rabelais stand?

I have argued elsewhere that the comic spirit of his book
derives in a large measure from the festive abandon, role-reversal
and ambiguities of the observances connected with folly,[15] and I do
not wish to rehearse these arguments again here. But it seems clear
at least that Rabelais's place cannot lie at the **bien-pensant** end of

the spectrum. Even if we disregard his constant references to food and drink, his **loquacitas, scurrilitas** and **immunditia**, we cannot fail to notice that the preface of his first book is addressed to people who spend their time (or would like to be thought of as spending their time) in reading light literature, hunting, courting ladies (and recovering from the results of successful courtships) and similar foolish pursuits. His heroes are great builders (what better example of 'edificare magna; edificare sumptuosa; edificare delectabilia' could there be than Thélème?) and great travellers; Panurge's quest provides a thinnish pretext for a voyage which might otherwise seem to be undertaken **ex sola curiositate.** Panurge's desire for marriage **propter delitias** may be unequivocally foolish, but Gargantua recommends it **propter generationem prolis** and as a means of self-perpetuation in this world (**Pantagruel** 8), and even the virtuous Hippothadée allows it **propter vitationem fornicationis** (**Tiers Livre** 30) - all foolish and unworthy reasons by the strictest canons of judgment. Maistre Alcofribas, Rabelais's alter ego, describes himself as an 'abstracteur de quinte essence' - a quintessentially foolish occupation - and he has clearly spent many a wasted hour among the useless byways of learning,[16] while his audience is defined as being 'de séjour' (**Pantagruel** 1) (if not 'folz de séjour', **Gargantua** Prologue), sitting around the barrel being fed with 'belles billes vesées' from the 'cerveau caséiforme' of the narrator (**Gargantua** Prologue).

Panurge is, no doubt, the most obvious of the fools on display. Indeed, the ringleader's part is one he plays with gusto. But we may wonder whether his uncrushable optimism is not, in its way, also a kind of wisdom. I have written elsewhere of the many ways in which he resembles both the court or kept fool and the Lord of Misrule or fool-society master of ceremonies.[17] But it is perhaps worth mentioning another characteristic he shares, this time with the medieval and early sixteenth-century stage fool - his irrepressible phallic exuberance. The **Satire of the Thrie Estaits,** again, includes an interlude in which a fool courts a lady by methods very similar to Panurge's in the 'dame de Paris' episode (though with better success), and in the same play Folie, just before delivering his sermon, alludes to the disturbing effects of the proximity of a 'fair las, with the sating goun' and proceeds to make the most scandalous insinuations about her. (There is no such character on stage, unless one of the allegorical figures from an earlier scene is still looking on - Dame Chastitie perhaps, who has been much ill-used in an earlier interlude. The lines may, of course, be addressed to a chosen 'victim' in the audience.) Such excitability is, no doubt, another sign of **stultitia.** But it too is a kind of folly which has its appointed place in the scheme of things. As Erasmus points out in the **Praise of Folly,**

> What is it, I ask you, which begets gods or men - the head, the face, the breast, hand or ear, all thought of as respectable parts of the body? No, it's not. The propagator of the human race is that part which is so foolish and absurd that it can't be named without raising a laugh. There is the true sacred fount from which everything draws its being, not the quaternion of Pythagoras.

Determination to marry in the face of all contra-indications is another kind of necessary folly - necessary, that is, if the human race is to be carried on: 'Just tell me please', says Folly, 'What man would be willing to offer his neck to the halter of matrimony if he applied the usual practice of the wise man and first weighed up its disadvantages as a way of life? . . . If you owe your existence to wedlock, you owe the fact of wedlock to madness, and can see how much in fact you owe to me'.[18] Albergati develops this passage at length, stressing the low-comedy aspects of the married state (**La Pazzia,** B v).

Geiler von Kaysersberg's remedy for the 'follies' of the married state is sexual abstinence: he interprets the Pauline text 'uxorem habere tanquam non habere' in a very different way from Rabelais's authorities (**Tiers Livre** 35):

> Beatiora sane coniugia iudicanda sunt: qui sine filiis procreatis sive prole contempta continentiam pari consensu servare queunt. O (dicis) est hoc uxorem habere tanquam non habere: Durum est verbum illud. Esto: durum sit: non tamen diu durat. Si diu duraret: durum forsitan esset. Sed non diu durat: quod breve tempus est. Non igitur frustra hoc verbum premisit prudens Apostolus: ut duritiam facti molliret brevitate momenti: quia tempus breve. Rogemus dominum.[19]

The austerity he recommends would no doubt be appropriate in a world nearing its end: but in a world with hope for the future, the 'folly' of constantly seeking to perpetuate one's genes (which biologists now tell us is the foundation of all animal behaviour) is clearly part of a larger pattern of wisdom.

It seems to me to be a serious misreading of Rabelais's work (and even of the **Tiers Livre** considered in isolation) to present it as a series of moral tableaux in which a single fool (Panurge) ignores repeated admonitions and calls to repentance from various representatives of wisdom. The whole of Ecclesiastes I, 15 does, it is true, read, 'Perversi difficile corriguntur et stultorum infinitus est numerus', but it is not by chance, I feel, that only the second half of the text has become proverbial. Popular comedy does not, in general, concern itself with the correction of the 'perverse'; that is the business of the sermon. The world of Rabelais's fiction is a world where all the characters, and the narrator and readers, are to some extent fools. It is a world of 'folz legistes' (**Pantagruel** 10), 'folz medicins' (**Quart Livre** 1), 'folz poetes' and 'philosophes resveurs' (**Tiers Livre** 18), as well as of idiots, mutes and wearers of cap and bells. Folly and wisdom are reversible, as in the seal of the **Mère-Folle** of Dijon, whose motto reads 'Sapientes stulti aliquando' and also 'Stulti aliquando sapientes'.[20] Reading Rabelais, we are temporarily liberated from 'ghastly good sense', from that 'pensée pratique' which, according to Michael Baraz, 'réserve au fou une place toute petite et périphérique'. 'Pour elle', he continues, 'la folie est un phénomène totalement aberrant, dont il faut réduire l'influence autant que possible'. Rabelais's writing, on the other hand, 's'engage dans la direction diamétralement opposée: elle entreprend de relier la folie à tout ce qui existe'.[21] The sense of scope, of space and freedom which Rabelais's writing gives, the quality which led Hugo to speak of his 'rire énorme',[22] and Flaubert to call him 'sans fond, infini, multiple' as well as 'sacro-saint, immense et extra-beau'[23] is related, I feel sure, to his apprehension and expression of that ancient maxim, **stultorum numerus infinitus.**

Carol Clark   Balliol College. Oxford

NOTES

1. The Douce Portfolios in the Bodleian Library, Oxford, contain a large number of sixteenth and seventeenth century prints relating to fools and folly. Most are in portfolios 133 and 142, but there are others scattered throughout the collection. 142/241-251 reproduce eighteenth-century drawings of the insignia of the **Mère-Folle** of Dijon, one of the best-known sixteenth-century fool-societies. It ceased to meet in the seventeenth century, but its banners, seals etc. were kept as

curiosities. Two of the seals bear the motto 'Stultorum numerus infinitus'. See also Douce 133/503, 142/91 and 460.

2. I discuss this point in **The Vulgar Rabelais** (Glasgow, 1983), pp.79-80.

3. For the publishing history of the **Ship of Fools**, see C. Schmidt, **Histoire littéraire de l'Alsace,** Paris, 1879 (reprinted Nieuwkoop/B. de Graaf, 1966), vol 2, pp. 340-45.

4. On Geiler, see Schmidt. ibid. vol 1, pp.335-461 and (for bibliography of the **Navicula**), vol 2, pp. 381-382. This bibliography is not complete; the **Navicula** was reprinted as late as 1572, at Lyon, with the old subjects newly engraved.

5. Holbein's drawings for the **Praise of Folly** show Folly in a pulpit. They are reproduced in the Folio Society edition of the text.

6. **La Pazzia** was published anonymously in several editions between 1540 and 1560 at Bologna, Venice and Rome (see J.E. Alden, **European Americana,** vol 1). The attribution to Albergati (by Melzi in his **Dizionario di opere anonime e pseudonime di scrittori italiani**) is dubious, for Albergati published no other vernacular works and none of his surviving writings are of a facetious character (on him, see **Dizionario biografico degli italiani,** pp.621-23). But it has been accepted by the British Library and so followed by other cataloguers. There are brief references to **La Pazzia** in Croce, **Aneddoti di varia letteratura,** vol 1, pp.329-30, and in E. Armstrong, **Ronsard and the Age of Gold,** p.139.

7. Douce E.1.6/393. I do not know the exact date of this print but the characters are wearing sixteenth-century costume.

8. Some (e.g. E.1.4/9) have the legend 'Tu quoque'.

9. 142/256.

10. 142/352.

11. **Materialien zur Kunde älteren englischen Dramas,** XLIV (1914), pp.89, 97-98.

12. 'Sermon joyeux et de grant value à tous les foulx qui sont dessoubz la nue', in Viollet-le-Duc, **Ancien théâtre françois**, vol 2.

13. J.-P. Jacobsen, **La comédie en France au moyen âge**, p.63.

14. In **Les joyeusetez, faceties et folastres imaginations**, Paris, Techener, 1829-34, vol 8.

15. In **The Vulgar Rabelais**, passim.

16. See G. Defaux, 'Rabelais et son masque comique: **Sophista loquitur' (Etudes Rabelaisiennes XI.** 1974) for an extended consideration of Maistre Alcofribas as learned fool.

17. **The Vulgar Rabelais**, pp.76-77, 86-89, 126-27.

18. **The Praise of Folly**, Penguin Classics, p.76.

19. **Navicula**, ch 51.

20. See Douce 142/246; also 142/193 and 213. I reproduce this seal on the back cover of **The Vulgar Rabelais**.

21. M. Baraz, **Rabelais, ou la joie de la liberté**, Paris, 1983. p.117.

22. 'Les Mages', in **Les Contemplations**, Book VI.

23. 'Sans fond', etc.: letter of 26 August 1853, to Louise Colet. **Oeuvres**, Club de l'Honnête Homme, vol 13, p.399. 'Sacrosaint', etc.: letter to Ernest Feydeau, late 1867: ibid. vol 14, p.388.

ROUGH JUSTICE IN RABELAIS

John Parkin

Rabelais's interest in popular justice is clear: characters such as Anarche, Picrochole and the Ecolier Limousin are subjected to such comic and spontaneous punishments as are visited countless times on others in the form of exaggerated threats: Baisecul will be decapitated if he lies in his statement to the court (**Pantagruel** 10), Gargantua will be subjected to perpetual din should he fail to return the bells of Notre-Dame (**Gargantua** 19), the audience to the **Gargantua** and **Pantagruel** prologues are menaced with ulcers, disease and death should they fail to enter into the spirit of the tales. In addition Rabelais seeks from literature and history retributive anecdotes such as the tale of doctor and surgeon beaten by their clients (**Tiers livre** 34), the humiliation of the Empress Beatrice in Milan (**Quart livre** 45) or the revenge of Frederic Barbarossa who forced the Milanese on pain of death to pluck one by one a fig from an ass's genitalia (ibid.). Despite the inequity of many of these real or imagined acts, that Rabelais believes in a transcendent moral order emerges often enough (e.g. via the faithful vision of paradise recounted by the dying Raminagrobis), and despite the author's satires of legal practice, the account of the pacification of Dipsodie and the speeches by Pantagruel at the Parlement de Myrelingues reveal a confidence that human justice can in its institutional practices yet be inspired by and take account of the sublime justice of God.

But where is God's justice in the guttersnipe stunts of Panurge (**Pantagruel** 16), the violent dismemberment of enemies in the clos de l'abbaye de Seuillé (**Gargantua** 27), the drowning of the Parisians (**Gargantua** 17), or the drowning of the sheeptraders (**Quart livre** 8)? For such acts of rough justice enlightened humanism provides no model and I aim in this paper to draw on Bakhtin's interpretation of the carnival in Rabelais to explain their humour and the relevance of moral judgments to them.

The punishment scene which Bakhtin analyses most fully is the Basché sequence in **Quart livre** 12-15,[1] where the Chiquanous are subjected to merciless flogging in a faked series of marriages in which the folk custom of exchanging light blows at weddings (**souvenirs de noces**) is surreptitiously converted into a genuine punishment of social enemies. Thus the punishment has both symbolic and real meanings: it involves ritual gestures characteristic of a rite of passage, but is also an attack on an abominated foe. The scene is structured in terms of both satire and parody: a satirical cadre is established when an unnamed raconteur explains how legal agents deliberately enrage the recipients of summonses beyond endurance in order to sue them later for assault. Rabelais transposes this anti-social practice into the fiction of **Procuration** island where the inhabitants simply earn their living by being beaten, then we encounter the Basché stories where the parody is sealed via all the carnival elements listed by Bakhtin and by the curious regeneration which the maimed Chiquanous and their henchmen undergo. They do not behave as enemies within Basché's castle but are courteous to him, apologetic to his retainers, and they praise him on their return to their master the prior of St Louant. This and the self-condemnation of the Chiquanous are enough to obscure the moral issue on which the satire is based, moreover none of the reactions makes psychological sense either: they must be interpreted as symbolic gestures leading to a conclusion which is paradoxically amicable and positive, despite the injuries received and the deliberate deceptions perpetrated:

> Ainsi départent. A demye lieu de là, Chiquanous se trouva
> un peu mal. Les records arrivent à l'Isle Bouchard,
> disans publicquement que jamais n'avoient veu plus homme
> de bien que le seigneur de Basché, ne maison plus
> honorable que la sienne. Ensemble, que jamais n'avoient
> esté à telles nopces. Mais toute la faulte venoient
> d'eulx, qui avoient commencé la frapperie. Et vesquirent
> encores ne sçay quants jours après.
>
> De là en hors feut tenu comme chose certaine que
> l'argent de Basché plus estoit aux Chiquanous et records
> pestilent, mortel et pernicieux que n'estoit jadis l'or de
> Tholose et le cheval Séjan à ceulx qui le possédèrent.
> Depuys feut ledict seigneur en repous et les nopces de
> Basché en proverbe commun.[2]

As well as resolving an injustice, the whole incident has become proverbial in local folklore.

Rabelais evokes carnival quite clearly in this episode: it is mentioned (B580; Jii80), fake weddings are an attested carnival stunt[3] and the comic beatings are called in **Quart livre** 15 a **jeu de jeunesse**. They are. The **jeunesse** (the group of young unmarried) were the organisers of carnival entertainments in traditional society and their corporate activities stimulated the parodic atmosphere of carnival, sustained its rules and traditions, and ensured, during carnival-time, the arraignment of such social enemies as the Chiquanous. These practices have been widely studied by modern social historians[4] but the category of **folklore juridique,** as parallel to official law, has been long discerned in the public denunciations, mocking gestures and defilements visited on guilty members of a community: especially noteworthy are the ancient traditions of the burning of effigies, charivari (a paramusical din created especially at night), and the ride on the ass (the victim often facing backwards).[5]

This folklore pattern, though unofficial and structured within carnival liberties, retains an ethical dimension: the victims (traditionally widows and widowers remarrying younger spouses, adulterers, prostitutes, wife-beaters, henpecked husbands, blacklegs, tax-collectors, unpopular landlords or preachers etc.) are punished with good cause and in terms of values often enshrined in official morality and law. Indeed E.P. Thompson concludes[6] that charivari belongs to a period when the people were not alienated from the law, an impression supported by Saintyves who notes that it was retained in various societies as a popular punishment for adultery long after this had ceased officially to be a crime.[7]

Clearly this raises problems for Bakhtin's notion of the carnival: does he not see it as a 'temporary suspension of the entire official system with all its prohibitions and hierarchic barriers' (op. cit. p.89), as a time when 'the authority of the official realm of Church and State is suspended with all its norms and values' (p.259)? Modern social history has refuted this[8] and it is curious that rather than analyse carnival in terms of a social dialectic, and as therefore underrun with contradictions, Bakhtin should idealise it in terms of his dubious category of laughter as a universal philosophical form which disappears from high culture as of the seventeenth century (q.v. Bakhtin p.67). The contradictions of carnival reside in its disruption of social order which yet seeks to guarantee the social order, the replacement of piety by profanity but only in accordance with a piously revered religious calendar, the violent unrestraint allowed in personal and group behaviour which yet imposes constraints on other groups or particular victims, a lifting of taboos to strengthen taboos;[9] its laughter, again complex, is compounded of a general hilarity which lowers inhibitions and invites everything, including one's own serious identity, to be parodied, and a positive satire aimed at the destruction of social evil, ensuring the reconstruction of the community and its collective security.

Several **jeunesse** groups appear in Rabelais's stories, one of the most obvious being Villon's **diables** who (q.v. Bakhtin pp.263-5) exact a comic punishment on Tappecoue (**Quart livre** 13): one could also mention the **moinetons** at Seuillé and, in that they are a loosely organised set of fun-loving bachelors, the Pantagruelistes themselves.[10] An example simpler insofar as having an exclusively festive function is the group of **compaignons** momentarily surrounding Panurge in the Latin Quarter pranks of **Pantagruel** 16. The stunts performed by them are punitive, involve mild tilts against legal and academic authority, desecrate the church with obscenity, force haughty women to run naked through the streets, and carnivalise the area converting it into a place of celebration where normal life and serious study are impossible. It is significant that the punishments can be vicious (Panurge whips page-boys in the street), mortal even (several passers-by die of the disease stemming from his **tarte bourbonnaise**), but also that they belong to the context of student festivity, whose licence was traditionally tolerated by the local authorities,[11] and that the victims' reactions can be joyous:

> Quand il se trouvoit en compaignie de quelques bonnes dames, il leur mettoit sus le propos de lingerie et leur mettoit la main au sein, demandant: 'Et cest ouvraige, est-il de Flandre, ou de Haynault?' Et puis tiroit son mouschenez, disant: 'Tenez, tenez, voyez-en cy de l'ouvraige; elle est de Foutignan ou de Foutarabie', et le secouoit bien fort à leur nez, et les faisoit esternuer quatre heures sans repos. Cependant il pétoit comme un rousin, et les femmes ryoient ... (B242; Ji306)

The outspoken satire is limited to occasional shafts at the Sorbonne (blunted in Rabelais's re-editions) but the assorted pranks conspire to mythologise Panurge as the lovable rogue of folk-legend whose subversion of officialdom embodies his public's repression, their resentment of it, and their sublimation of this resentment.

Hence there exist ambiguities even in such a simple sequence as the pranks of Panurge. To see him as some kind of sadistic persecutor is surely erroneous,[12] it being important to define Panurge as an assemblage of literary types (rogue, clown, fool) relevant not to an individual psychology but a group psychology which imposes these roles on the **jeunesse** leader in a response to rituals demanded by the group: his behaviour is not determined by motives springing from the complexes of his own psyche. The rituals are demanded at certain times and in certain places, hence Panurge here inhabits the **chronotopes**[13] of student carnival. Their humorous effect depends on a mood which modern psychologists relate to the group in whom 'the sheer enjoyment and excitement of ongoing play activities may produce endless bouts of laughter, even though nothing is really "funny"[14] and which Bakhtin historicises as 'the laughter of all the people . . . universal in scope . . . directed at all and everyone, including the carnival's participants' (Bakhtin, p.11).

Like the laughing women, the scapegoats of charivari could yet enjoy their punishment, given its ritual status: arraigned as social enemies they could yet emerge as the amused observers of their own humiliation. Similarly their tormentors both flaunted private morality (invading privacy, thieving, beating) whilst upholding public morality (demanding loyalty and respect for the family, the **natio**, the clan, the village, the town). On the basis of this ambiguous morality (which sanctions puerile taunts, legitimate outrage, frank hooliganism) a satiric laughter can coexist with the gleeful mood of carnival: via punitive jests the group ostracises a member and reasserts itself at his expense. When as in **Pantagruel** 16 the punishments are farcical, justice becomes suffused in a parody of official forms of life; when the attack is fiercely motivated, satire is the dominant mode and judgments are demanded of the bystander. In his academic satire ('oingnit theologalement tout le treilliz de Sorbonne' etc. (B239; Ji302)), Rabelais here makes assumptions which a popular audience would not share and applies cues to which he could not guarantee a response, but the structure whereby a parodic inversion of social behaviour and a satiric imposition of ethical judgments operates dialectically in Panurge's role situates him nonetheless in the tradition of popular carnival. In these terms the description of Panurge with which the chapter opens is significantly ambiguous:

> Malfaisant, pipeur, beuveur, bateur de pavéz, ribleur s'il
> en estoit à Paris; au demourant, le meilleur filz du
> monde (B237; Ji301)

One man's **jeunesse** leader is another man's thug.

The punishment I wish to consider now retains comparable patterns: it is that visited by Panurge on the **haulte dame de Paris** in **Pantagruel** 21-2. This involves the defilement and humiliation of a woman who is the object of Panurge's desire up to the point where he tires of the game of seduction and decides to vent his spleen on her. As a tale it fits into the immense Medieval tradition of adultery **contes** and this is a key reason again to exclude all readings based on individual characterisation: for Glauser it is evidence that Panurge is psychologically inadequate:

Panurge ne parle que d'amour et de mariage, parce que par
sa nature et ses actes, il est incapable d'aimer et de se
marier[15]

a line extended by D. Losse:

Panurge is obsessed with the physical aspects of love
. . . (unwilling) to transform simple or unrequited love
to reciprocal love[16]

and Defaux generalises this approach, which implies that rather than
composing a comic eulogy of Panurge, Rabelais is composing a moral
allegory condemning him:

Dominer autrui par l'intelligence et par la parole ne
suffit pas à Panurge. Il lui faut encore exalter son
orgueil par l'humiliation et l'avilissement de son
semblable . . . . Triompher n'est rien, il lui faut de
surcroft détruire la victime, lui faire sentir
l'irrémédiable étendue de sa défaite et lui inspirer le
sentiment d'une déchéance indélébile. Les victimes de
Panurge sont à jamais des victimes.[17]

No. In this scene Panurge is individuated merely in order for
Rabelais to introduce the structure of the adultery **conte** which
requires not groups but three individuals: lover, lady, husband
(absent here, though existent). Thus Panurge has another identity
imposed on him, that of lustful seducer antithesis of the pining
courtly lover, but the outcome of the tale, in which the woman is
put to shame by being drenched with the urine of more than half a
million dogs, is again a carnival punishment organised by Panurge
for public entertainment.

This type of story in which a woman's marital virtue is
assailed by a celibate (normally) has no predetermined outcome. The
lover may be willingly accepted, the husband cuckolded and sometimes
beaten (e.g. in the **Fabliau de la Bourgeoise d'Orléans**), the lover
may be frustrated and sometimes beaten (e.g. in **La surprise et
fustigation d'Angoulevent,**)[18] the woman may be tricked into
surrendering against her will (**Decameron** 3.6), the woman may accept
the lover but be punished by a vengeful husband (**Cent Nouvelles
Nouvelles** 47) etc. The problem of twisting new patterns from such
oft-used threads required ingenuity in the story-teller and the key
source of comedy is the variation between respect for marital
fidelity (codified in official morality) and the expression of

sexual desire (codified in a counter-morality operating in both courtly and **gaulois** traditions).[19]

The tales are carnivalesque in several ways. Firstly they belong in their telling to contexts of relaxation: the **veillée**, the evening fireside, the feast day, the meal, the tavern, the village green, the pilgrim's journey - **chronotopes** where serious preoccupations are at a distance if not forgotten. Secondly the unpredictable cross-penetration of moralities which they embody bears analogy with the parodic values and behaviour of carnival. Thirdly they concern some of the very misdeeds which were punished during carnival, a re-enactment being sometimes performed before the victim's eyes: van Gennep recounts how this current of popular dramatisation, parallel to the **farces** and **soties** of the Middle Ages, might punish by display an aged bridal couple, an adulterer, a couple living in sin, a cuckold, an unmarried mother, a wife-beater, a beaten husband, a drunkard, a debauchee or a fool (as the woman represented feeding fried leeches to her husband instead of applying them live to his body).[20] The public humiliation of the victim is mitigated again by ritualisation, comic intent and carnival glee. The victim often made gestures of approval, applauding the performance, offering money or drinks to the revellers, nay even participating with good will in the prank aimed against him. Such participation was symbolic: a neighbour or a straw dummy could suffice. Actually to resist could involve further punishments, however, and a recourse to official justice might well prove fruitless[21] for to negate the spirit of carnival festivity was a social crime.

The morality underlying the punishments, like that operating in the stories, is, though genuine, fraught with contradictions, for seemingly innocent people (newly-weds, bachelors) might well be punished, whilst all parties to the adulterous triangle (seducer, mistress, cuckold) were fair game. Each time a **conteur** draws attention to popular justice, rites of passage, or the **chronotopes** of carnival he is highlighting the relevance of this tradition to his stories. Thus in **Cent Nouvelles Nouvelles** 53 we have the preposterous account of two couples married by mistake to partners of dissimilar age (old man to young woman, young man to old woman): they thereby become classic targets of a charivari and the **jeunesse** group, whilst preparing the **chaudeau**[22] to be offered them, confirm the legality of the marriages, thus guaranteeing further grist to the festive mill. Philippe de Vigneulles' **Cent Nouvelles Nouvelles** 40 recounts the tale of the cuckolded husband who punished his wife by burning her buttocks over a fire: the carnivalesque enters via this absurd (though violent) punishment, the publication of it ('En

fut tel bruict que la chose en fut divulguée par la ville'),[23] and
the pre-Lenten setting: the adultery is discovered and the
punishment exacted 'au gras temps devant Karesme, voir, au temps de
paix'.[24] The ladies who judge the tale of Jehan de Saintré's
treacherous mistress recommend a series of ostracising and demeaning
punishments for her:

> 'J'en dy . . . c'on la devroit bannir de toute bonne
> compaignie.'
> 'J'en dy . . . c'on la devroit lyer sur un ane, le viz
> devers la queue, et mener par la ville à grant derision.'
> 'Je dy ... que telle dame devroit estre despoillee toute
> nue dez la ceinture en amont et toute reze, puis oindre de
> miel, puis menee par la ville afin que les mouches li
> courissent et la picassent.'[25]

These are all popular, ritual punishments incongruous to the setting
and hence imagined rather than inflicted. The carnival is evoked by
the general laughter which accompanies their description ('Lors n'y
eust là dame ne demoiselle que toutes n'en rissent'):[26] in reality
the woman is punished with a courtly delicacy which provides a
highly artistic contrast.

In the **dame de Paris** scene we have a similar contrast of
courtly or at least aristocratic manners, and base popular
punishment. As carnival involves social levelling, so this is
appropriate. The different **chronotopes** employed (society reception,
Sunday Mass, holiday streets) reinforce this contrast as do the
variations in Panurge's wooing speeches where flattering rhetoric
('C'estoit à vous, à qui Pâris debvoit adjuger la pomme d'or, non à
Venus' (B261; Ji328)) stands against frank obscenity ('Doncques pour
gaigner temps, bouttepoussenjambions' (ibid.)). Rabelais has
already satirised the traditional courtly lover as an **amoureux de
karesme** (B260; Ji327). Panurge, the carnival swain, adopts this role
principally for comic purposes: the traditional gestures of the
lover (conferring gifts, composing poems, languishing in
desperation) are travestied by him and at the turning-point of the
story, when his desire becomes contempt, Rabelais draws attention to
the mask:

> Adoncques Panurge tourna son faulx visage, et lui dist:
> 'Vous ne voulez doncques autrement me laisser un peu
> faire? Bren pour vous!' (B264; Ji331)

It is intriguing to note that the woman bears a mask too, and a more psychological one. In order to contrast Panurge's exteriorised behaviour, Rabelais grants her an interior personality through which, via surreptitious gesture, thought pattern and deliberate ambiguity of expression, her feminine coquettishness emerges. Like the majority of women in adultery contes she is prepared to compromise herself, and thus merely pretends to rush to the window for help against Panurge's advances, drools over the jewels he describes, and cries out 'toutefoys non trop hault' (B264; Ji331) when he tries to kiss her. Essentially though, these remain stylistic exercises in contrast rather than the means by which Rabelais justifies Panurge's revenge: in particular it is interesting to examine her thoughts as involving a dialogue between the two roles (faithful wife, deceiving adulteress) which she is adopting:

> Pensoit: 'Ce bon bavart icy est quelque esventé, homme d'estrange pays: je ne recouvreray jamais mes patenostres. Que m'en dira mon mary? Il se courroucera à moy: mais je luy diray qu'un larron me les a couppés dedans l'église, ce qu'il croyra facillement'. (B262; Ji329-30)

The faithful wife would tell the truth, but the lustful woman intimidates her into silence so as to leave the door open for Panurge, who with only a little more persistence would complete the seduction.

Instead he opts for a punishment, in which the woman's personality is obliterated: from a self-reflective character she is converted into a ritual victim displayed before the townsfolk of Paris, her own laughing chambermaids and Panurge's lord Pantagruel. The **chronotope** is carnivalesque, so also the spectacular nature of the punishment, the violence, the scenic parody: from being a procession of the faithful following the cross to church[27] the scene becomes a rout of dogs chasing the woman to her home which they then befoul. The simulated hunt is an attested form of charivari and van Gennep gives examples of the use of animal masks by such revellers.[28] The victim might be pursued out of the town or else to his or her dwelling which might then be defiled as in Rabelais. The mutilation of animals frequently characterised this type of insult: horses' heads, dead cats, calves' feet might be deposited;

> Un amoureux éconduit se vengeait en suspendant un animal mort à la porte et faisait une traînée de résidus de charbon de la maison de la fille à la rivière ou à un

'cloaque immonde':   même punition pour les filles
acariâtres ou revêches.[29]

These are May-time rites which invert the flowers or trees presented
by fortunate lovers, and while being an act of personal vengeance
they publicise a grudge and form a sanction of **folklore juridique.**
The problem is once again the moral validity of this sanction.
Not after all an adultress, the **dame** rejects Panurge with ample
justification: a woman should shun importunate **rustres**, whilst to
welcome them might well in turn invite a charivari. Is Panurge then
guilty of sadism, or is the scene simply a representation of
carnival anarchy where Rabelais 'carries the Pantagruelian
assumptions to the extreme statement that life is copulation with
anybody at any time'?[30] No; for the lady is not anybody, she is a
figure drawn from a specific literary tradition, nor is this any
time: it is one of the **chronotopes** of carnival. Panurge is not a
sadist, he is a reveller enacting a travesty of courtship which he
concludes with traditional forms of punishment in which, once more,
respect for life, property and propriety are inverted. The woman,
having failed somewhat hypocritically to respond in terms of this
comic pastiche, is punished for her shrewish refusal to play the
role which Panurge, literary tradition and Rabelais's
carnivalisation of social mores lay open for her.   Apparent
innocence is no defence against rough justice: on carnival days all
passers-by risked being besmirched with filth as all newly-weds must
anticipate a charivari. It is an attested May-time custom that a
married woman be freed to quit her husband and rejoin the **jeunesse**
on a temporary basis,[31] but she resists Panurge and the vindictive
act is sanctioned by the counter-morality of carnival. She does
after all threaten Panurge with alarming violence herself ('N'estoit
pour un petit, je vous feroys coupper bras et jambes' (B260; Ji327))
and fantasises a ritual beating for him ('Je appelleray le monde et
vous feray ici assommer de coups' (B261; Ji327)). Moreover to
demand an equitable correspondence between crime and punishment
would be to read the text as a judicial allegory when it is a tale
of illicit love underrun with carnival elements, and also to ignore
the ritual element in carnival justice which limits its effect to
that part of an individual which he abstracts from community life:
and in this episode, as Bakhtin remarks, it is community life that
is enriched (a new river is created from the dog's urine), whilst
the private life of the individual (momentarily highlighted during
the story) ceases to exist once she leaves the street.
Along with this dislocated morality various other important
ambiguities emerge, amongst which, via the birth of the river, we

see regeneration arising from destruction and thus epitomising carnival parody as Bakhtin has theorised it. Similarly the fact that the dead bitch was in heat parodies the woman's barely concealed sexuality. It is the denial of this element in her nature that is exorcised in the soiling of her doorway but the vilification is a purification: the woman disappears; and her humiliation is Panurge's exaltation: a further triumph in a further role. The woman is at once Panurge's personal victim and the communal scapegoat: we are invited to enjoy her discomfiture and thus side with the Pantagruelistes, for such humour, whilst attacking a victim, should consolidate and reassure the community from which the victim has been expelled.[32] The parody renders any tragic catharsis irrelevant, for having toyed with the psychological problems of adultery Rabelais discards these themes from the tale and his conclusion belongs to another tradition entirely: not the adultery **conte**, nor the carnival **Schwank**, but the explanatory folktale which tells of the origins of natural features.[33]

Thus the mini-theory I am propounding[34] is one whereby the rough justice meted out in Rabelais's texts can be associated with the ritual punishments of carnival exacted by **jeunesse** groups as a gesture of combined ostracism and socialisation. Its violence reflects the spectacular and extreme forms of behaviour which carnival encourages, its victims are selected from a typology of social enemies (some of whose misdeeds may be quite serious, others extremely trivial) while the frequent discrepancies between punishment and crime may be explained both by a mood of glee which encourages, rewards and is sustained by incongruity, and by the ritual side of the custom which reduces the victim to a symbolic target of odium, whilst allowing his humanity to express itself via self-mockery and willing participation in the rite of punition.[35] Not all these patterns apply to any particular scene, it being Rabelais's intention to do more than merely present tableaux of carnival castigation: however in varying combinations these features do emerge more richly and expressively in him than in comparable writers, this in part explaining his superiority over them. The vitality of his texts is generated by this very refusal to be systematic or predictable, and by the interpenetration of this popular spirit into a story vindicating a transcendent morality personified by Pantagruel.

Applying the mini-theory to the sheep-trader sequence we can see how Rabelais uses once more the **chronotopes** of carnival (the entire pilgrimage of the **Quart livre** is one, more particularly in chapter five the festive meeting with co-nationals): there is a significant shaft of anti-Tridentine satire (on the 'chapitre

general des Lanternoys'), then we experience a long exchange of
insults between Dindenault and Panurge in which there are frequent
references to adultery and cuckoldry and to carnival punishments
appropriate to them:

> - Je te demande (dist Panurge) si, par consentement et
> convenence de tous les élémens, j'avois
> sacsacbezevezinemassé ta tant belle, tant advenente, tant
> honeste, tant preude femme, de mode que le roydde dieu des
> jardins Priapus, lequel icy habite en liberté, subjection
> forcluse de braguettes attachées, luy feust on corps
> demeuré, en tel désastre que jamais n'en sortiroit,
> éternellement y resteroit, sinon que tu la tirasses
> avecques les dens, que feroys-tu? ...

> - Je te donneroys (respondit le marchant) un coup d'espée
> sus ceste aureille lunetière.   (B553; Jii48-9)

Initially violence is pre-empted by Pantagruel, and toasts are made
in reconciliation (the normal socialising gesture) but trouble
flares up again as Dindenault vaunts his sheep using the style of
bonimenteur so frequent in Rabelais, whilst Panurge heckles him.
Then when the trick is played the roles are reversed, for as
Dindenault drowns, Panurge becomes the carnival priest whose **sermon
joyeux** employs the topoi of the vale of tears and the glories of
paradise to console his murdered victims. Again standards of equity
are grossly distorted as a private grudge becomes a public display,
however with exteriorisation comes again a socialisation as Panurge,
victim of greedy mercantilism, becomes Panurge, organiser of the
revels, whilst Dindenault with his entire company becomes a
scapegoat, a reified symbol of popular contempt, his private
subjectivity, which flickered into life during the arguments,
annihilated. The conclusion is again arbitrary: Panurge might as
easily have been Dindenault's victim, for successful swindlers can
be made attractive,[36] whilst as far back as the end of **Pantagruel**
Rabelais has converted his carnival inquisitor into a potential
victim of popular justice via his projected marriage which will lead
to his being hen-pecked and cuckolded. After all, any folk-hero can
degenerate into a popular buffoon[37] and the purpose of such scenes
is not to establish logical continuity, but comic variety. The
death of Dindenault like the vilification of the **dame** serves to
exorcise the negative elements within the scene, allowing Rabelais
and his readers to pass on to the next episode with a clean
conscience.

We may object, but to demand that normal standards of equity apply in rough justice is like demanding that Rabelais's stories be logically consistent. We may insist, but, like the youth who stands aside from the carnival revel, we will be isolated from the spirit of the occasion, from the appropriate conventions, from the fullest reading of the text, and may fall victim to Rabelais's assaults on agelasts. Official punishment rites should punish; they should also reform, deter and repress, and these varying functions create their own contradictions:[38] popular punishments exhibit in addition elements of comic display and parody which thrive on an incongruity of punishment and crime. But a distorted morality remains a morality, and without it carnival would become anarchy and its celebrations meaningless.

Futhermore Rabelais jogs our (clean) conscience with such pious phrases as that quoted by Frère Jean (**mirabile dictu**) after Dindenault has drowned: **'Mihi vindictam'** (B561; Jii58; cf Romans 12.19). Having responded as he wishes, we are thus invited to examine our response, and its relevance to Rabelais's serious anti-Tridentine or anti-Scholastic satires. And Bakhtin, having discovered, then universalised the regenerative quality of parodic humour, finds himself unable to handle Rabelaisian satire effectively. Instead of seeing it as a functional element in virtually all of Rabelais's humour, he marginalises it as a sub-category ('Only a few secondary characters and episodes of the novel's last books can be described as satirical' (p.141)) which he then fits into an unconvincing historical pattern vindicating Rabelais's cultural progressivism:

> This old authority and truth pretend to be absolute, to have an extratemporal importance . . . their representa-tives . . . are gloomily serious. . . . They do not see themselves in the mirror of time, do not perceive their own origin, limitation and end; they do not recognize their own ridiculous faces or the comic nature of their pretensions to eternity and immutability. And thus these personages come to the end of their role still serious . . . Kind master Rabelais deals with these dummies pitilessly, cruelly, but merrily. (pp.212-3)

But the victims Rabelais destroys are not always representatives of a dying order, moreover the order was far from moribund, and sixteenth-century carnival sought in many ways to celebrate it. In literature as in society attacks on lechery, pedantry or hyprocrisy are satirical topoi: they create the divisions which are then parodied in the punishment tableaux; but when Rabelais inserts Renaissance motifs into these tableaux this is not enough to explain their meaning, otherwise Basché would be a hero of Humanist law and Dindenault an enemy of Gallicanism.

Instead of constructing factitious historical patterns around phenomena, a dialectical analysis must explain them in terms of contradiction and negation: thus as the violent humour of childhood negates an alien adult value system, so the violent humour of the sadist negates human respect and love, so the violent humour of carnival, with its insults, scatology, threats and beatings, is a negation of that mixture of taboos and restraints constituting social life: polite restraint becomes noisy clamour, private property is abundantly shared, even stolen, sober dress becomes extravagant or obscene costume, violent abuse replaces mutual respect and rough justice judicial equity. But this parody of social life bears within itself the negation of that negation: the resurrection of social responsibility renewed and reinvigorated - this is the essence of Bakhtin's most important contribution to the study of its humour.

The reinvigoration was a violent process: the symbolic cry of 'death to you'[39] need not be merely symbolic; rough justice could become lynch-law; carnival revelry revolution.[40] But by allowing group loyalty to determine one's pattern of behaviour one freed oneself from individual preoccupations: the fear of death was obliteratred in collective hilarity; unorthodox behaviour forsook the restraints and repressions to which one was subject. To fit these patterns to the development of sixteenth-century history and thence to Rabelais as interpreter of that history must be the task of his students, but it is one which cannot be performed satisfactorily by the mere analysis of his expressed thought otherwise the comic dynamism of Panurge would be defeated by the normative commentaries of Pantagruel in the **Tiers livre,** and this never happens. For the problems posed by Panurge's own degeneration to the level of scapegoat, the butt of the kind of **Schwank** he himself performs in **Pantagruel** involves more than a negation of the Humanist/Evangelical values which Pantagruel expounds when arguing with him. Important though they are, these values do not enshrine the moral implications of popular justice and cannot therefore be seen as circumscribing the text with ideological norms by which its comic action be judged. Such norms have a function (even in the mouth of Frère Jean) but not an exclusively edifying one, and it is carnival ambiguity not codified morality that is the clearest analogue of Rabelais's creativity.

To deny that Rabelais's satire has any ideological dimension is preposterous. It is important, as Bakhtin says, to avoid reducing comedy to either a purely negative satire or else a gay fanciful recreational drollery deprived of philosophical content: to do so substitutes a reified dichotomy for a dialectical interrelationship. Unfortunately Bakhtin tries to encapsulate this interrelationship in invented notions like a creative laughter peculiar to Renaissance literature from which Rabelais emerges as people's **choregus** (p.474). Such rhetoric merely idealises folk-humour, the Renaissance and Rabelais. Far from being radically opposed to Medieval ideology, the mentality of vast sections of Rabelais's humbler contemporaries was totally penetrated with it, hence his (albeit parodically expressed) disgust with the Parisian people, and impatience with the cult of the saints, idolatry and pilgrimage. Such attacks penetrate into his comic punishments, but these remain no less a re-enactment of folk ritual generic to carnival, whilst also reflecting a self-conscious literarisation of these rituals whereby, for instance, the **dame de Paris** is recognisably characterised and her treatment identifiable with archetypal parodies of courtly love enshrined in the **fabliau** and **nouvelle** traditions.

When Rabelais metes out the unjust justice she and his other victims endure, he enmeshes the reader in a number of contradictory patterns challenging him to adopt a consistent position notwithstanding the threat to his moral integrity. He must adapt so as to render the destructive humour acceptable to himself, but the comic destruction and the rough justice occasioning it are in their social roots creative and positive: so also perhaps in its psychological implications is the adaptation freely performed by the responsive reader. It has been the task of Western criticism to reconstruct the no more clearly defined models (wise ignorance, Christian folly, **Pantagruelisme**) on whose basis Rabelais invites him thenceforth to pattern his serious life.

John Parkin

University of Bristol

Acknowledgement

Research for this paper was funded by the British Academy to whom I express thanks.

NOTES

1. q.v. M. Bakhtin, **Rabelais and his World**, pp.196-208. This and all other references are to the M.I.T. Press edition (trans. H. Iswolsky, Cambridge, 1968).

2. References are to the following two editions. Rabelais, **Oeuvres complètes**, ed. J. Boulenger, Pléiade, (designated B). Rabelais, **Oeuvres complètes**, ed. P. Jourda, Garnier, 2 vols, (designated J). In this instance: B583-4; Jii84.

3. q.v. A. van Gennep, **Manuel de Folklore Français Contemporain**, I,iii (Paris, 1947), pp.1066 and 1079, and C. Gaignebet, 'Le Combat de Carnaval et de Carême', **Annales**, 27 (1972), 313-45 (p.334).

4. q.v. van Gennep, op. cit., also N. Davis, **Society and Culture in Early Modern France** (London, 1975), Yves Bercé, **Fête et Révolte** (Paris, 1976) and P. Burke, **Popular Culture in Early Modern Europe** (London, 1978).

5. q.v. V. Alford, 'Rough Music or Charivari,' **Folklore**, 70 (1959), 505-18, R. Maunier, **Introduction au Folklore Juridique** (Paris, 1938), P. Saintyves, 'Le Charivari de l'Adultère et les Courses à Corps Nus', **Ethnographie** (1935), 7-36.

6. 'Rough Music: le Charivari anglais,' **Annales**, 27 (1972), 285-312.

7. art. cit. p.36.

8. q.v. Bercé (op. cit. p.36): 'La fête ne s'identifie pas au désordre, elle n'est pas un retour anarchique des instincts. Elle est un contre-ordre et le contre-ordre est encore un ordre'.

9. q.v. Burke, op. cit. p. 201.

10. e.g. in the Dipsodian War or the satire of Homenaz. Davis's similar identification of the Thélémites (op. cit. p.123) seems audacious however.

11. q.v. L. Petit de Julleville, **Les Comédiens en France au Moyen Age** (Paris, 1885), p.6, C. Haskins, **Studies in Medieval Culture** (Oxford, 1929), p.33, H. Rashdall, **The Universities of Europe in the Middle Ages** (Oxford, 1936), vol.III, 431-2.

12. q.v. G. Defaux, **Pantagruel et les Sophistes** (The Hague, 1973): 'C'est peut-être dans ses rapports avec la femme que se révèlent le mieux ses talents de persécuteur sadique et son ambition de dominer' (p.176).

13. This term is drawn from the French translation of Bakhtin's **Esthétique et Théorie du Roman**, tr. D. Olivier (Paris 1978), part III, and is defined as 'la corrélation essentielle des rapports spatio-temporelles telle qu'elle a été assimilée par la littérature' (p.237).

14. P. McGhee, **Humor, its origin and development** (San Francisco, 1979), p.125.

15. **Rabelais Créateur** (Paris, 1966), p.146.

16. 'Thematic and Structural Unity in the Symposium of Rabelais's **Tiers Livre**', **Romance Notes**, 18 (1974-5), 390-405 (p.402).

17. op. cit. p.174.

18. q.v. **Les Joyeusetés, Facéties et Folastres Imaginations de Caresme Prenant**, (Paris, 1829-1831), vol.12.

19. q.v. R. Nelli, **L'Erotique des Troubadours** (Toulouse, 1963), p.216: 'Il était généralement admis que les plus honnêtes dames pouvaient aimer si elles aimaient . . . pour elles l'amour annulait toutes les morales' and **Ordonnances generales d'amour** (Antwerp, 1574): 'Deffendons les iniures verbales, permettons toutefoys aux marys, pour la primauté et puissance qu'ils ont dessus leurs femmes, de se pouvoir rire et gausser d'icelles en toutes compagnies, à la charge que leurs femmes s'en pourront revencher' (**Joyeusetés** etc., vol.14, p.6).

20. op. cit., p.1070ff.

21. q.v. J.-C. Margolin, 'Charivari et Mariage Ridicule', in **Les Fêtes de la Renaissance** vol.III (Paris, 1975), 579-601, recounts how a Toulousain widow in 1478 sued the **Jeunesse** for

placing corpses against her door; she lost the case and was fined a round of drinks.

22. This is a brew revolting in taste and appearance offered to the bridal couple often in a chamber pot and with accompanying **brouhaha** after the **nuit de noces:** q.v. van Gennep, **Manuel** I.ii, pp.560ff.

23. P. de Vigneulles, op. cit., ed. C.H. Livingston (Geneva, 1972), p.185.

24. op. cit. p.183.

25. A. de la Salle, **Jehan de Saintré,** ed. J. Misrahi and C. Knudson (Geneva, 1967), pp.305-6.

26. ibid. p.306.

27. q.v. Bakhtin's treatment of the scene, pp.229ff.

28. q.v. Thompson, art cit. p.287, and van Gennep, **Manuel,** I.iii, p.918.

29. q.v. van Gennep, **Manuel,** I.iv, p.1556 (a Languedoc custom).

30. R. Paulson, **The Fictions of Satire** (Johns Hopkins Press, 1967), p.83.

31. q.v. Nelli, op. cit. pp.31-2.

32. This process of 'foolmaking' as a means of eliminating a social deviant is discussed in O. Klapp, 'The Fool as Social Type', **American Journal of Sociology,** 55 (1950), 157-62.

33. q.v. S. Thompson, **The Folktale** (New York, 1946), p.9.

34. This term is used out of deference to P. McGhee, 'On the Cognitive Origins of Incongruity Humor', in **The Psychology of Humor** (ed. J.H. Goldstein and P. McGhee, New York, 1972), where he argues for 'the development of alternative mini-theories designed to account for limited aspects of the total humor process', this process having thus far defied all 'global unidimensional theories' (p.62).

35. This behaviour-pattern is analysed by W.H. Martineau, 'A Model of the Social Functions of Humor', in **The Psychology of Humor** (ed. cit.), 124. Relevant historical detail is in Bercé, op. cit., c.1, 'Les violences de la fête'.

36. q.v. S. Thompson (op. cit. p.165) on **Cheats**: Herodotus's tale of the triumphant thief contains brilliant examples of destruction and regeneration symbols (ibid. p.171).

37. ibid. p.190.

38. Burke (op. cit. p.197) notes how official authority adapted carnival procedures so as to popularise public executions.

39. q.v. Bakhtin p.248 on the Roman carnival as described by Goethe.

40. Bercé (op. cit. p.51) recounts how the actor playing Judas in carnival processions ran frightful risks. Deaths were commonplace in carnival battles and the growth of political action out of carnival festivity is the main subject of Le Roy Ladurie's **Le Carnaval de Romans** (Paris, 1979).

ΑΓΑΘΗ ΤΥΧΗ

LES HORRI
BLES TAROTZ
& prouessesespous
tables de PAN
TAGRVEL
roy des Dipsodes,
composes par M.
ALCOFRIBAS
abstracteur dequin
te essence.

M. D. XXXIIII.

Dufresnoy

INDEX
of principal proper names.